# TRANSFORM YOUR MSME² MNC

Amazon #1 Bestseller

# CMA PANKAJ JAIN

Worldwide Published by
Pendown Press

**PENDOWN PRESS LLP**
An ISO 9001 & ISO 14001 Certified Co.,
**Regd. Office:** 3767A, Kanhaiya Nagar,
Tri Nagar, Delhi-110035
**Ph.:** 8130886000, 9650072927
**E-mail:** info@pendownpress.com
**Branch Office:** 1A/2A, 20, Hari Sadan, Ansari Road,
Daryaganj, New Delhi-110002
**Ph.:** 011-45794768
**Website:** PendownPress.com

**Edition:** 2025

**ISBN:** 978-93-6338-011-0



*Layout and Cover Designed by* Pendown Graphics Team
*Printed and Bound in India by* Thomson Press India Ltd.

# DEDICATED

To my **Isht,** The Ultimate **Guru, Gurus,**
**Coaches, Parents, Family, Friends**
and **Entrepreneurs.**

"When India speaks of becoming self-reliant,
it doesn't advocate a self-centred system.
In India's self-reliance; there is a concern
for the whole World's happiness,
cooperation and peace."

~Hon'ble PM Shri Narendra Modi

# CONTENTS

□ □ □ □

# PREFACE

An Aatma Nirbhar Bharat is well set to take back its ancient status and glory in the arena of International Trade once again. As the global order gets reset, the ancient 'Trusted Relationship' based Business models of Indian Merchants who played a prominent role in global trade become highly relevant for Entrepreneurs of Micro, Small and Medium Enterprises (MSMEs).

Indian MSME Entrepreneurs can easily leverage these principles to transform into Global MNCs in the post-Covid Global Order.

In my Vanijya Sadhna for over the last 33 years, I have gained a reputation as a Global MSME & Realty Strategist following these eternal principles. And that is exactly what I am sharing in this book.

MSME is an inclusive term that encompasses a broad spectrum of businesses. Even mobile cart vendors, small shopkeepers and housewives running small home-based enterprises fall in the purview of MSMEs.

With all my experience, I can safely say that every MSME owner aspires to or dreams of transitioning into a Multinational Corporation (MNC) at some point in their entrepreneurial journey.

While many people may see this as mere wishful thinking, I can assure you that with the right guidance and following the right path, every MSME has the potential to become an MNC.

However, the time taken to make this transition may be different for every Enterprise, depending on their typical situation. With the abundance of opportunities available in the present world scenario, it is the best time for MSME owners to take a leap of faith powered by targeted guidance to scale up their business and make themselves Aatma Nirbhar (Self-Reliant) while spreading their empire globally.

So, stay with me through the following pages and stay excited as I share with you the secrets to navigating the challenges of transitioning from an MSME to an MNC smoothly, safely and speedily.


~Jai Jinendra

CMA. Pankaj Jain.

> The world is your market, why limit your imagination only to India?
>
> ~ C.K Prahlad's line that inspired Ratan Tata

☐ ☐ ☐ ☐

# Why This Book?

As I shared earlier, this is the best time to manifest the dream that every MSME owner holds in their heart to scale up their business to the highest level and take it global.

This brings us to the next logical question: What is it about MNCs that every business owner aspires to be one?

**The reasons everyone aspires to be an MNC are because:**

- ➢ An MNC has a global presence and, hence, a broader market penetration.

- ➢ It operates at a much larger scale of business.

- ➢ Due to its worldwide presence and bigger markets, an MNC has higher profit earnings.

- ➢ An MNC has a high potential for growth due to its larger scale of operations and a wider playing field.

- ➢ An MNC has a unique and recognizable Brand Identity & Value.

**However, transitioning to an MNC from an MSME is not easy. The challenges are many. And that is where this book comes in.**

- ➢ In this book, we will first learn what an MNC is and what its advantages are.

- ➢ Then, keeping the world business scenario in perspective, we will thoroughly understand the Indian context of global business.

➢ Next, we will identify and understand the 4 types of enterprises.

➢ Having understood all the above, we will embark on understanding the new Global Business Model post the Covid-19 Pandemic and its lingering impact.

➢ Finally, I will share with you the critical steps to successfully transition & transform your Enterprise from an MSME to an MNC.

In keeping with the endeavour of being self-reliant, I am on a mission to guide 10,000 MSMEs and launch them firmly onto the trajectory of global dominance by becoming an MNC.

This book is a part of my service journey to fulfil this mission.

> Finance is all about business, and business is all about people."
>
> ~ CMA. Pankaj Jain

☐ ☐ ☐ ☐

# WHO AM I?

Quoted above is the Key Learning from 27 years of my corporate experience working in senior-level Finance and Business Leadership roles...

Ok, so having read so far, I am sure there is another question crowding your mind. "Who is Pankaj Jain, and why should I listen to him?"

**So as you know by now, My name is Pankaj Jain.**

An alumnus of IIM Calcutta, I am a CMA, CS, AMT, and a Certified Independent Director. I am also the creator of the Msme2MNC Model.

Filled with the vibrant spirit of entrepreneurship fortified with over 33 years of diversified experience across a broad spectrum of industries, I have a proven track record of turning around the financial position of several companies through dynamic initiatives and helping them achieve exponential growth even in challenging times.

While working at top-level corporate positions as a VP, CFO, CEO, & Director, I have successfully led the growth of reputed business houses such as Super Seals, IAP, ERA Infra, and the Logix Group to the next level against all odds.

I have managed numerous strategic business initiatives involving Venture Formation, Business Modelling, Strategic Financial Planning, Corporate Alliances, Demergers, Divestments, Cost Optimization, Business Restructuring, Capital Structuring, Corporate Governance and Corporate Financing for successful businesses with global footprints.

I have also successfully raised funds for projects (including mega infrastructure projects under Public Private Partnership) with a cost of over Rs. 15000 crores from domestic and foreign sources.

Additionally, I am associated with many socio-economic initiatives in various capacities, including Founder President/ Chairman of the Indian Society of Management Accountants, Infra and Real Estate Foundation, Young Entrepreneurs Network, Indian RERA Forum, Bhartiya Global MSME Forum and have the privilege of being a mentor to many startups to help them achieve sustainability and scalability in their businesses.

I live, work and inspire others with this simple philosophy—

**"Dream Beyond Imagination… Desire Within Limitation."**

**My driving force is the belief that "If Others Can Do Why Not You?"**

**My magic mantra for winning at business is to Collaborate, Collaborate & Collaborate, which I firmly believe in.**

We do not grow in isolation; we are stronger when we pool our resources and combine our strengths and core capabilities.

**I am honored and humbled to share with you some of my accolades…**

➢ Recipient of GOLD Medal for Best Performance.

➢ Regular Jury member of Asia One, a Dubai-based leading global media group that evaluates ratings for the Top 100 brands in India, Asia, and the world.

➢ Mentor to many Startups, Entrepreneurs and MSMEs with the objective of helping them to achieve SUSTAINABILITY, SCALABILITY and SUCCESS in their Businesses in the Global Arena.

➢ Guest faculty to leading Business Schools, Professional Institutes and Business Forums.

➢ Advisor on Boards of various Institutions and Independent Director of Listed Companies.

Also, let me share with you my Investment Outlook in brief:

Collaborating with entrepreneurs to achieve SUSTAINABILITY, scalability and Success of their businesses with GLOBAL Footprints...

➢ **Mission:** Build self-sustainable institutions responsible for sustainable INCLUSIVE growth of the UNIVERSE...

➢ **Interest Areas:** Tech-based solutions for the Environment, MSME sector, Infra and Real Estate.

**You can always stay in touch with me @**

pjainonline@gmail.com

+91 9312213765

www.CmaPankajJain.in

in.linkedin.com/in/cmapankajjain

youtube.com/channel/UCZBtd6I17_5ula1nyliekSA

twitter.com/cmapankajjain

www.instagram.com/cmapankajjain/

facebook.com/public/cmapankajjain

www.slideshare.net/search?q=pjainonline

> "Navigating your business to the next level is not merely a choice; it is your responsibility."
>
> ~ CMA. Pankaj Jain

# Is This Book For Me?

In our series of questions, let's address the third critical question in your mind right now.

I am certain you are wondering, "Is this book for me?"

**Yes, this book is an absolute must-read for you if you are:**

➤ An Aspiring Entrepreneur.

➤ An Entrepreneur, including a Startup Owner.

➤ A Business Owner.

➤ A Professional in any Domain.

➤ A Bureaucrat.

➤ A Politician.

➤ An Academician.

➤ A Student.

➤ Or even an MNC looking for the next level of growth.

The world post-pandemic is poised at a critical juncture.

New ways of interacting and doing business have evolved, and only those who adapt and keep pace with the fast-changing global scenario will be able to survive and thrive.

If you have a vision for being self-reliant and running a successful and profitable global enterprise. **It is time to act Now!** And you are holding the Key to that doorway to success in your hands. So let's dive deep into it...

From my extensive experience and deep research into the challenges and concerns of **MSMEs** I understand that while things may differ a bit from sector to sector but nearly all of them have a similar set of challenges that they are SEEKING Solutions for...

➤ You inevitably face bottlenecks in your business and want to have a sound system in place to Bounce back higher and faster.

➤ You want to beat the competition and Stay ahead of the crowd.

➤ You want to make your business a Brand to reckon with.

➤ You want to have a Dashboard of your business at your Fingertips.

➤ You want to establish a Model for achieving Sustainable Inclusive Growth for your National Economy.

➤ You want to Run your Business without you.

➤ You want to Make Money even when you Sleep.

➤ You want more Quality Time for you and your Family.

➤ You want more Happiness in your Life.

If you answered YES to any, many or all of these, then this book is definitely for you!

> "Our Greatest Glory is not in never Falling,
> but in Rising Everytime We Fall."
>
> ~ CMA. Pankaj Jain

# THE CORE AREAS OF TRANSFORMATION– PERSONAL TRANSFORMATION

Your journey of transforming your MSME into an MNC will involve transformation at the deepest level in 3 core areas.

1.  Personal Transformation

2.  Enterprise Transformation

3.  Business Transformation

One level of transformation is your Personal Transformation

## Personal Transformation

Your personal transformation begins with understanding and discovering yourself.

1.  **Knowing Yourself**

    a.  The first step is understanding who you are because YOU are the most important person in your Life. Everything, every relationship, and every circumstance exist because of you. Of course, there are external factors that impact your Life, but everything is driven by you. How you respond to these external factors is what creates your Life.

    b.  The most important question to understand is, why are you here? Each of us is a unique being with our own set of skills, interests and impact. What one person brings to the table, the other perhaps cannot. So understand that no matter your age, gender, status, education etc., each of us serves a purpose on this planet, so never doubt your worth.

**c.** What is your purpose? Once you understand that you have a purpose to fulfil, the next logical step is to identify what that purpose is. True success will find you once you follow and live your purpose.

**d.** Life is such that it never moves in a straight line; therefore, it is guaranteed that at some time or the other, you might get thrown off track. At such times you must have something that reminds you to get back on track. So it is important to identify what brings you back to your purpose.

## 2. Balancing your Soul, Mind and Body

For sustainable success, it is important that all your actions must be aligned with your purpose. This basically means that your desires, thoughts and actions must be one. Only then will there exist a balance of your Soul, Mind & Body. To give your best, it is important that you must be healthy spiritually, mentally and physically.

## 3. Make it a Core Purpose of your Life to Serve Others

Success and prosperity come to us and stay with us only when our intent and purpose move from being merely self-centred to being selfless. To grow big, we must think big. We must have the intent to serve others while creating abundance for ourselves.

Before you embark on your business transformation, it is necessary to work on yourself, and the best way to work on yourself is -

## — Focus on yourself —

You are the result of your own

## THOUGHTS, WORDS & ACTIONS!

Nothing will ever change no matter how many homes, cities, businesses or employees you change; things will only change when your behaviour and actions change, and these will change only when your thoughts and words change.

I have a simple mantra for transformation that can truly give you global success-

# विश्व

It means the **WORLD**

**And if you look at it closely and understand deeper, what is the World made up of-**

**विश्व= वि + श + वृ**

**वि= विचार (Thoughts), श= शब्द (Words),
वृ= व्यवहार (Actions)**

To transform your business, you must first transform yourself, and two things are key to transforming yourself:

1.  **You must always have an open mind and an attitude toward learning.** When you have an open mind, you believe

anything is possible, and from this belief comes all creation and success. If you are not open to possibilities, you are limiting yourself, and a limited mindset is like a cage you make for yourself. You must greet every person and circumstance as a learning opportunity; even failure can teach you lessons on what needs to be avoided and what more needs to be done. We will talk about this more in the next point.

2.  **You must not fear failure and not let it stop you from taking action.** So many people I meet are hesitant to think and act big because they are afraid of failing. Here I have a radical piece of advice for you. Do not be scared of failure, do not shy away from it. Instead, embrace your failure. For who fails? Only those who try, and there is no way of winning and succeeding without trying!

**Therefore failure is something that no one can avoid. It is inevitable and is a part of every successful journey.**

Let me share with you a secret about dealing with failure. **Often uninvited guests will drop in at your house, you do not like it, but do you stop living in your home from the fear of these guests?** Do not run away from failure. Think of it like an uninvited guest; when that guest arrives on your doorstep, do you run out of your backdoor or hide in your room... No?

Instead, you open the door, put on your best smile (even if it is fake) and greet them, ask them to come in, offer them tea/ coffee and all courtesy but make sure they do not let them stay for too long. Soon you see them off at the door.

That is exactly what you do with failure, and neither do you run away from it. Nor do you let it stay and impact you for long. Some entrepreneurs I have seen let failure scar them for a long time; they stay rooted in fear and do not move forward. Failure is unavoidable, but it is not permanent. You learn from it and move on.

Therefore, let go of the fear of failure because when you let go of fear, you give your best and operate from a place of passion.

Now that you understand the importance and the basics of **Personal Transformation,** continue to work on yourself through the right routine of yoga, meditation, visualization, affirmations and reading the teachings of great masters and Gurus, as learning and growing are ongoing processes.

The second level of transformation is your Enterprise Transformation.

□ □ □ □

# Enterprise Transformation

What is even more important than business transactions is the vehicle of your business journey- your Enterprise.

*Enterprises are the growth engines of businesses and the economy.*

Therefore your business growth depends on the kind of Enterprise you choose to run. From my entire experience and research, I have surmised that there are four types of enterprises.

**A Person Driven Enterprise** is an enterprise that is dependent on its owner, and all decisions are taken by the owner. If you choose this type of Enterprise as your business vehicle, then it is like riding a **Motorcycle**; while you may be able to manoeuvre your way in & out of challenges, you will not be able to face weather changes, and also you will be able to grow only to a limited level as your vehicle can only handle so much.

**A People Driven Enterprise** is one where there is an owner and a team of professionals guiding it. This kind of business vehicle can be said to be an upgrade to a Car. You can travel faster & safer, and there is more scope for growth compared to a person-driven Enterprise.

**A Process-Driven Enterprise** is one where along with the owner and the team of professionals, there are standard processes also in place to handle all necessary activities and operations. Using this business vehicle is like having a **Train** at your disposal.

You can grow quite far and fast, and there is a lot of potential to grow.

**A Purpose-Driven Enterprise** has everything that all the above three have, but here the purpose is the boss, you, your people and your processes are driven by the passion of that purpose. It is like flying an **Airplane,** and this is the most powerful growth engine. There is no limit to your potential, the World is your sky, and you can reach your destination superfast.

Therefore if you have to grow and make your mark as a successful India-based MNC like Tata, Mahindra, Birla, Infosys, Bharti, HDFC, ITC etc., it is imperative that you identify your purpose of doing business and then ensure that every word, thought and action is aligned toward that purpose.

Let's Build PURPOSEFUL Enterprises which can be GLOBALLY Sustainable, Scalable and Super Successful.

> Let's Build PURPOSEFUL Enterprises which can be GLOBALLY Sustainable, Scalable and Super Successful.

□ □ □ □

# A PURPOSE-DRIVEN MNC

> "It's only when companies are clear about their purpose, have clearly communicated it, and it is understood by the team that companies can achieve both unity of effort and distributed decision making."
>
> ~ Marc Koehler

Now that we have been talking for quite some time about transforming your business into an MNC, it's important to understand what exactly an MNC is and why everyone aspires to be one.

> "A multinational corporation (MNC) is a company that has business offices and operations in at least one country (or more) other than its home country. These operations are often managed from a central office headquartered in the home country."
>
> Here I want you to clearly understand that an enterprise that is merely exporting goods to another country or even many countries does not qualify as an MNC.

Now the question arises, why does every business owner wish to transform their business into an MNC?

The answer is simple but manifold:

- ➢ An MNC has a **Large Scale of Business Operations.**

- ➢ Due to its large scale of business, an MNC has **Higher Profit Earnings.**

- ➢ It has a **Wide Global Presence.**

- ➢ Since it has a global presence, it offers a **Higher Potential for Growth.**

- ➢ An MNC also has a **Popular Brand Value & Recognition.**

Here I'll let you in on a secret—there is something even better than being an MNC. **It's a Global MNC.**

An MNC is one that simply replicates the business model it uses in its own country in all the other countries of its operations, whereas a Global MNC is one that tweaks its business model to suit the needs and sensibilities of its local area of operations. **Such enterprises think global but act local.** This helps the local people identify with these companies, leading to their success.

## Purpose is the Fuel that Drives the Wagon of Success

However, even beyond a Global MNC exists a type of Enterprise that succeeds and becomes a brand beyond all benchmarks of success!

This Enterprise is a **Purpose-Driven MNC.** A purpose-driven MNC is one that does not merely focus on generating business and financial success; rather, it has as its core value

and mission something beyond numbers. It has the intent and desire to serve people and contribute to society.

One of the greatest examples of a purpose-driven MNC exists in our own country itself. It is none other than the Tata Group.

The founder of this group, Jamshed ji Tata, stated in writing that their purpose of doing business was to contribute to the economic growth of India and to give back to the people. And that is what has been driving them till today.

They are a group worth billions of dollars, but that is just one of their success criteria; they are known and recognized for reasons beyond that.

# REVIVING INDIA'S ANCIENT GLORY OF GLOBAL TRADE WITH THE NEW BUSINESSMODEL

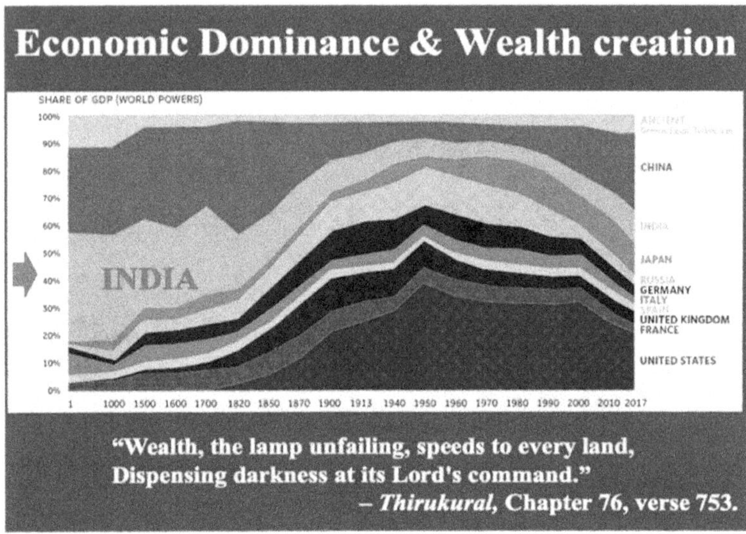



At one point in time, Ancient India had nearly 40% share in Global Trade.

If you wish to embark on your journey of transforming your MSME into an MNC, the time is now.

Post-pandemic, the field of opportunities is wide open and inviting. The World has shrunk due to technology, and India has moved up in the rankings of countries and their ease of doing business.

You can join the revolutionary list of businesses that are striving to revive India's traditional trade glory and dominance. Just to give you a little context, if we were to look at the trade history of various prominent countries such as the USA, China, Italy, France, Germany, the UK and India for the last 1000 years, we would find some unexpected things.

Look carefully at the picture below, which depicts the timeline on one axis and the trade share on the other.

You will find that at one period of time, India held the lion's share and dominated the world trade. Also, you will notice that India has been a consistent player throughout, with a significant contribution. With the current business scenario in our country and the World, **it is the right time to begin transforming your MSME into an MNC and contribute to India's economy and restore its Business Glory.**

## The New-Age Business Model

However, we operate in a new age today, and the new-age dynamics of business have changed radically. Today the World is poised on the verge of an ecological challenge where we might lose the planet we live on. Climate change, environmental pollution and other hazards are real threats.

The pandemic has taught us that anything catastrophic can happen and upset our cart at any time. We have all been through the challenging times of the pandemic, so I really don't need to elaborate on it any further.

*So here's a simple deduction- if there is no environment, obviously, there will be no enterprises.*

We are all aware of the time-tested QCDS Model of doing business, which emphasizes Quality, Cost, Delivery & Service.

However, with the changing times, another criterion has been added to the mix.

This new criterion is the ENVIRONMENT.

**Henceforth only those enterprises will succeed and survive who care for the environment's welfare and will operate in an eco-friendly, sustainable manner, no matter the industry.**

| **New-Age EQCDS Business Model** |
| :---: |
| Environment = = = = = Protected |
| => No. 1 Priority for Every Business |
| Quality >>>>>>>>>>> Up |
| Cost <<<<<<<<<<<<< Down |
| Delivery = = = = = = = = = = On Time |
| Service = = = = = = = == = On Demand |

If protecting the environment in all possible ways that your business permits is not your priority, it will indeed be difficult for your business to survive, leave alone thrive {It can even be things as small as not printing anything unless necessary, using zero plastic, having an eco-friendly building, rain-water-harvesting etc.} everything has an impact.

> "Take care of the earth, and she will take care of you."
> ~ Traditional Proverb

As you continue to transform at a personal level and enterprise level, you must simultaneously work on transforming your MSME into an MNC through the Business Transformation Practices listed below, which I will share with you in detail in the forthcoming chapters.

# CHAPTER - 1

# From Local to Global:
## Developing an MNC Mindset for MSME Success

> "An MNC Mindset is the critical difference between playing small & going global"
>
> ~ CMA Pankaj Jain

Often the next big goal of many micro, small and medium enterprises (MSMEs) is to venture as multinational corporations **(MNCs)** and achieve global success. **While the vision is great, it is crucial to understand that simply entering international markets will not serve the purpose.**

While it may be relatively easy to foray into international markets, the real challenge is sustaining yourself in those markets. Building a global presence requires thriving in those markets and the biggest challenge you will face is the difference in the core culture of each market. What works in Italy will not work in the USA or an Asian country such as Singapore. **Navigating cross-cultural challenges is key to leaping from an MSME to an MNC, and it all begins with developing the right.**

Business leaders often prioritize gaining a larger share of foreign markets through strategies like language expansion, office expansions, and currency support. **However, these efforts represent only a portion of the overall equation.**

As **MSMEs** embark on the journey of globalizing their operations, they need to develop an **"MNC Mindset"** to reach their full international potential.

To achieve an MNC Mindset, leaders must focus on integrating global thinking into their corporate cultures and daily operations.

**It involves adopting a global perspective and understanding the complexities of operating in diverse cultural, economic, and regulatory environments.**

Here are a few key points to consider when aiming to cultivate an MNC mindset:

1.  **Global Awareness:** Before you enter any markets, ensure that you are informed about global trends, market dynamics, and geopolitical developments that could impact your business. This includes understanding cultural nuances, consumer preferences, and local business practices in different countries.

    Incorporate market intelligence tools and data analytics to continuously monitor and assess global trends, enabling proactive decision-making and the ability to swiftly adapt to changing market dynamics.

2.  **Adaptability:** The most critical tool to navigate cross-cultural challenges and preferences is to embrace flexibility and adapt to diverse cultural norms and business practices. Develop a proactive mindset that embraces new approaches. It will enable you to respond promptly to evolving market dynamics and seize opportunities for growth and expansion in different international markets. Understand that what

works in one country may not work in another. Be open to learning and adjusting your strategies accordingly.

3. **Cross-Cultural Competence:** While awareness of and the willingness to adapt to cross-cultural changes is one thing, putting your willingness & understanding to work is the real challenge. You will need to develop cross-cultural competency to thrive in a global sea of competition.

   It begins by being appreciative of different cultures & learning to coordinate your efforts with people from varying backgrounds. To promote an inclusive and diverse work environment you will need to invest in cross-cultural training to boost your organisation's cross-cultural competence. Cultural sensitivity, empathy, and effective communication skills are also essential for building strong relationships and collaborative partnerships.

4. **Strategic Thinking:** To go from a limited set of possibilities to an unlimited playing field, you must think beyond national boundaries and consider how your company can leverage global opportunities. This would mean exploring potential markets, partnerships, and collaborations that align with your business objectives and developing a long-term vision for expanding your presence internationally.

5. **Risk Management:** Understanding and exploring opportunities is just one side of the picture. It is also important to understand the risks associated with operating in different countries, such as political instability, economic fluctuations, and regulatory challenges. Implement effective risk management strategies to mitigate potential threats and protect your business interests. Developing robust contingency plans and regularly reassessing and updating

your risk management approach can ensure business resilience and minimize potential disruptions.

6. **Talent Management:** Attract and retain a diverse pool of talent with the skills and expertise needed to operate globally. Foster a culture of inclusion and provide opportunities for professional development and cross-cultural learning within your organization. Establish effective talent management strategies, such as succession planning and mentorship programs, to groom future leaders and ensure a strong pipeline of skilled professionals capable of driving global growth and innovation.

7. **Ethical Conduct:** Uphold high ethical standards and adhere to local laws and regulations in each country of operation. Maintain transparency and integrity in your business practices to build trust with stakeholders across different regions. Additionally, prioritize corporate social responsibility by actively engaging with local communities and addressing environmental sustainability concerns, demonstrating a commitment to ethical conduct beyond legal compliance.

8. **Best Practices Sharing:** Develop efficient sharing of best practices across subsidiaries and borders. By building trust, sharing practices, and recognising opportunities, companies can enhance performance and competitiveness. Training programs and interactive learning occasions facilitate knowledge transfer. Promoting a learning culture and sharing experiences minimize mistakes, save time and costs, and improve problem-solving efficiency.

9. **Effective Communication in Global and Local Contexts:** Communication is critical to global success. The key is to effectively communicate across global and local demands.

Strike a balance between local adaptation and global standardization by finding solutions that align with global standards while meeting local operating and regulatory requirements. Understand diverse cultures and address their unique demands to bridge the gap between global and local contexts, facilitating effective communication and enabling harmonious collaboration. This will help to navigate the complexities of diverse markets while maintaining a consistent global identity and achieving sustainable growth.

10. **Acting on Emerging Opportunities:** Tailor your products or services to meet the specific needs of diverse markets by understanding global trends, identifying emerging markets, and assessing consumer demands in different regions. Conduct thorough market research, embrace agility, prioritize innovation and differentiation, invest in global talent acquisition, and foster a culture of continuous learning to successfully navigate the global marketplace.

11. **Building Trust Across Cultural Settings:** Understand different work styles and behaviours to effectively coordinate operations in diverse countries. Prioritize cultural sensitivity, open communication, and adaptability to foster trust among employees from various cultural backgrounds. This trust forms the basis for successful collaboration, knowledge sharing, and problem-solving, leading to enhanced coordination and success in global ventures. Valuing cultural understanding and trust-building helps navigate cultural boundaries and leverage the diverse perspectives within global teams.

Going global requires adaptability, agility, and a willingness to evolve in response to dynamic market conditions. Embrace change by fostering a culture that encourages innovation, experimentation, and continuous learning. Be open to new ideas, technologies, and market trends, and be ready to pivot strategies when necessary. Embracing change can help seize emerging opportunities, navigate challenges, and stay ahead in the global marketplace. It fosters a forward-thinking mindset that fuels growth and innovation.

Remember that developing an MNC mindset is an ongoing process that requires continuous learning, adaptation, and an open mindset. By embracing these principles, you can position your company for success in the global marketplace.

# CHAPTER - 2

# ESG for MSMEs —
# A Sustainable Route to Becoming a Global MNC

Comprehending Environmental, Social, and Governance (ESG) is important for small and medium-sized organizations, especially when seeking to step into worldwide markets. ESG practices like measures, guidelines, and procedures can help different groups maximize their fine contributions to society, governance, and the environment. It guarantees moral enterprise practices in these domain names. The importance of ESG for MSMEs is emphasized in this chapter, which also highlights how it could be used as a device for global growth through encouraging environmentally and socially aware commercial enterprise practices that benefit humans and the surroundings.

## UNDERSTANDING ESG

Environmental, Social, and Governance, or ESG, is a framework that assesses how organizations engage with their surroundings, treat humans, and make choices.

The environmental factor is involved with reducing pollution and the use of less water, energy, and different resources. Fair treatment of workers, customers, and employees, as well as community involvement, are all part of social considerations.

A company's decision-making, moral business practices, and legal compliance are evaluated by governance.

ESG mandates that companies give top priority to ethical behavior, open decision-making, and legal compliance. It acts as a thorough manual for ethical and sustainable corporate practices, highlighting the significance of reducing negative effects on the environment, advancing social justice, and upholding strong governance frameworks.

In simple words, ESG can be described as a set of practices (policies, procedures, metrics, etc.) that organizations implement to limit negative impact or enhance positive impact on the environment, society, and governance bodies.

## Can Small Businesses Use ESG?

Some small enterprises may think that only big companies can use the ESG framework for their growth. However, it's a misconception, **as ESG can also assist small enterprises in saving money, growing their business, and standing out from the crowd.**

## The Significance of ESG for MSMEs

For MSMEs, ESG is essential for several reasons.

- ➤ **First,** it helps with risk management by locating and resolving possible problems that could later have a negative effect on the company.

- ➤ **Second,** it increases the likelihood of attracting investment since investors are now more likely to give priority to businesses that exhibit strong ESG performance, which means more money for expansion.

➤ **Thirdly,** implementing ethical ESG practices helps establish a positive reputation for the company. It attracts partners and customers who respect social responsibility and the environment. Furthermore, ESG compliance aids companies in navigating and abiding by a variety of laws, particularly as they grow internationally.

➤ **Finally,** ESG stimulates innovation by pushing the creation of socially and environmentally conscious business practices. It results in fresh concepts and methods that are advantageous to the company as well as the planet.

## Tips for Small Businesses to Implement ESG

Adopting ESG practices by small businesses is a strategic tool for growth and competitiveness, going beyond compliance.

➤ **Environmental Initiatives:** Start with green projects like cutting back on resource use and setting up recycling schemes.

➤ **Social Responsibility:** For social responsibility, give equal treatment to employees and give community involvement and customer service top priority.

➤ **Ethical Governance:** Transparent choice-making, adherence to ethical ideas, diverse management, and legal compliance are all additives of moral governance.

I Implementing a complete ESG method consists of power conservation, recycling, truthful labour practices, community engagement, and moral governance. This can help MSMEs to become more competitive and open up growth opportunities.

## Attract and Retain Better Talent Easily

ESG commitment creates a positive work environment that makes employees happier and prouder, which attracts and keeps top talent. A company's attractiveness is further enhanced by emphasizing diversity and inclusion, which guarantees that every individual feels valued and welcomed.

## Let People Know About Your ESG Initiatives.

To display a business enterprise's dedication to sustainability, it is vital that ESG projects are conceived, implemented and showcased with transparency and accuracy. Effective communication increases visibility and positions the employer as one who cares whether it is through written reviews or social media. This openness raises staff morale while also fostering stakeholder trust.

## In Conclusion

ESG is essential for small companies looking to expand. It is a calculated move for future readiness, cost savings, and growth, not just about being morally right. Businesses can build a positive reputation and win the respect and trust of stakeholders and customers by making ESG a top priority today. It is not just good; it is essential for small businesses hoping to grow into respectable, profitable organizations..

# CHAPTER - 3

# The Triple Win Strategy
## Transforming MSMEs into Global Powerhouses

> ## THE TRIPLE WIN FORMULA
>
> A great thumb rule to always ensure success with service is the "Triple WIN Formula". Simply put, this formula means that for every transaction or decision you make, you should stop and think of how it impacts not just the two parties directly involved in the transaction but also the other parties (third parties) that it may impact.

**The Triple Win formula aims to create positive outcomes for three key stakeholders:**

➢ The business itself

➢ Its customers

➢ And the broader society or environment.

This formula takes care of the interest of third parties who are not a direct part of transactions between the two main stakeholders.

This approach of the Triple Win formula is very much relevant in today's business world, where businesses are more and more expected to be socially and environmentally sustainable while being profitable.

Let us see how MSMEs can adopt this concept to add more value to their transitioning into an MNC.

1.  **The First Win: Business Growth and Profitability**

    - **Innovation and Diversification:** For any business to grow, innovation acts as its lifeblood. It is important for your business to develop new products and services continuously. When we talk about innovation, we mean leveraging cutting-edge technology, entering untapped markets, or diversifying into related business areas. Innovation can lead to differentiation and open new areas for revenue.

    - **Market Expansion:** In this scenario of MSMEs transforming into MNCs, finding new global markets and expanding their reach are significant steps. It also means understanding and acquiring different cultural, legal, and business settings. Creating a new customer base involves understanding their needs and preferences.

    - **Achieving Operational Efficiency:** For any business to sustain and grow, streamlining operations is very important. It could involve things like optimizing supply chains, automating processes, and adopting lean business practices. Efficient operations lead to reduced costs, improved trust and reliability, better productivity and quality, and hence more profits.

2.  **The Second Win: Customer Satisfaction and Loyalty:**

    - **Providing Value and Quality:** To gain customers' trust and retain them, it is crucial to provide them with high-quality products, better services, and good experiences. You need to continuously listen to customer feedback and improve your offerings to match their needs.

- **Connect with Your Customers:** These days, you get several opportunities to connect with your customers through various digital platforms. Provide great customer service, build a community, respond promptly to their inquiries, clear their doubts, and much more. Using such practices, you can foster loyalty and trust in your brand.

- **Customization:** In global markets, there is no one-size-fits-all formula. You should find ways to customize your products and services to get a competitive edge.

3. **The Third Win: Social Responsibility and Environmental Sustainability:**

- **Sustainable Practices:** As a responsible business, you should implement eco-friendly practices such as applying for recyclable programs and using renewable energy resources. This is good not only for your environment but also for your business sales. Customers these days favor brands that are socially responsible.

- **Community Development:** It is highly recommended that your MSME contribute to communities so you can strengthen your brand reputation. To do that, you can support local initiatives, educate people around you about socially important matters, create jobs, or take part in charitable activities.

- **Ethical Business Practices:** It is of utmost importance to maintain high ethical standards in all aspects of your business. It may be implementing fair labor practices, ethical sourcing, and transparency. Such behavior will lead to long-term sustainability and a better reputation.

## How to Implement the Triple-Win Formula

➢ **Strategic Planning:** To get the best out of the Triple Win Formula, integrate it into your core business strategy. Set clear goals and objectives that align with all three stakeholders. And consciously review the progress.

➢ **Engage with Stakeholders:** One of the vital aspects of implementing this strategy is to keep continuous communication with each party, including employees, customers, and community members. You can get valuable insights for your business development by understanding their needs and expectations.

➢ **Work for Sustainability:** Consider the social and environmental impact of every business decision and action. Find ways to reduce any negative impact they create. This strategy should be integrated into the core of your business.

➢ **Cultural Sensitivity in Global Expansion:** Cultural sensitivity is a crucial aspect of gaining acceptance in case of global expansion. To gain a foothold in a new global market, you need to understand their cultural ethos, needs, and preferences and create your products, services, and business practices accordingly.

➢ **Regular Innovation:** Create an environment in your organization that encourages continuous innovation and creativity. It involves investing in research and development.

➢ **Corporate Social Responsibility (CSR) Initiatives:** Develop CSR programs that contribute positively to society. These programs should align with your company's values. These initiatives help enhance brand image and create strong relations with the community.

## In Conclusion

Implementing the Triple Win Formula into your business provides a strong framework for transitioning from an MSME to an MNC. You will build a successful global brand by focusing on all three aspects, namely business growth, customer satisfaction, and social responsibility. This strategy, apart from driving profitability, contributes to a better world. It creates a win-win-win scenario for the business, its customers, and society at large.

# CHAPTER - 4

# Engaging and Empowering People: The Key to Transitioning from MSME to MNC

## PEOPLE ARE POWER

When transforming your MSME into an MNC, the most critical aspect is its people. This transition is a journey that requires meticulous planning and attention to achieve your goal. However, with a focus on empowering people using the right strategies, it can be achieved.

**Before moving further in our discussion, let us understand why people are so important for any business.**

**It is not only products and services that define a business.**

The core of any business is defined by its people who put their creativity, expertise and skill into creating, developing, selling and supporting these services or products.

**Without people, a business is just an idea.**

So, it is quite crucial to empower your people- by giving them knowledge, tools, training and confidence to perform at the highest level.

In an MSME, employees often multitask as they are adaptable, flexible and involved in the business deeply.

## What does "Empowering People" Mean?

Empowering people means providing them with opportunities for growth and development. You can achieve this by conducting training programs, mentorship, or giving them more responsibilities.

When employees feel valued and become more capable, they will contribute more towards the business's success.

## So How can a Business Empower its People?

### Strategies for Empowering People

The business will need to navigate new markets, cultures, and regulations. Empowered employees will take on leadership roles easily, guide new team members, and help the business adapt to its new global environment.

**The most important aspects that come into play include the following:**

➢ **Training and Development:** Invest in your employees' skills. Conduct formal training programs, workshops, or online courses. The more skilled your employees are, the more they will contribute to the business.

➢ **Open Communication:** Encourage employees to share their ideas and feedback. This can lead to innovation and improvement, and it also helps employees feel valued and heard.

➢ **Recognition and Rewards:** Recognize and reward hard work. This not only motivates employees but also shows them that their contributions are appreciated.

➢ **Leadership Opportunities:** Provide opportunities for employees to take on leadership roles. This can help them develop new skills and prepare for the challenges of an MNC.

## Other Important Aspects

When empowering people, sharing and providing a positive, collaborative and supportive environment that helps them feel professionally accomplished. Creating and nurturing a conducive environment for growth and opportunities can help a business move in the right direction. These aspects include.

➢ **Sharing A Supportive Work Environment:** A supportive work environment motivates employees to take risks, innovate, and collaborate. Promoting a culture of respect, inclusivity, and teamwork will help in this direction.

➢ **Give Them Right Set of Tools And Resources:** Give employees the tools and resources they need to perform their jobs effectively. This could include the latest technology, access to relevant data, or even a comfortable workspace.

➢ **Encouraging Work-Life Balance:** Empowered employees are those who can balance their work and personal lives effectively. Businesses can support this by offering flexible work hours, remote work options, and understanding that employees have commitments outside of work.

> **Promoting Autonomy:** Empowering people often involves giving them the autonomy to make decisions related to their work. This shows trust in their abilities and judgment, which can boost their confidence and motivation.

> **Fostering a Sense of Purpose:** Employees feel empowered when they understand the bigger picture and how their work contributes to it. Communicate the company's mission, vision, and goals clearly and regularly to help employees see the value in their work.

> **Supporting Employee Wellness:** Physical and mental health plays a significant role in employee performance. Offering wellness programs and mental health resources and promoting a healthy lifestyle can contribute to overall employee empowerment.

## Take Your People Along

Empowering people is not just a strategy for business success; it's a necessity for any MSME looking to become an MNC. By investing in their people, businesses can navigate the challenges of expansion and growth and make the journey from MSME to MNC a successful one.

A business is only as strong as its people. Empower them, and they will empower your business.

# CHAPTER - 5

# The Secret Ingredient to Success: Focus on Value Creation

What makes venture capitalists or investors invest in certain businesses?

Why do customers purchase goods and services from a particular brand?

Why do employees prefer to work with one company over another?

The answer to all these questions lies in an essential business objective and that is **'Value Creation'.**

Investors invest in a business with the hope of making long-term financial value. Customers make buying decisions based on perceived value. And employees stick to a company for monetary value. Value creation is one of the core mantras of success. It is the foundational bedrock of business. It's what sets you apart from your competition, fosters customer loyalty, and gives a distinct identity and branding to your enterprise. It is the starting point of any and every business transformation.

## What is Value Creation?

To understand value creation, you must first understand value. In simple words, value is the measure of the worth of something.

It is not equivalent to price. Value can be in the form of saved time, reduced errors, increased productivity and so on.

**There are two primary types of values in business:**

1. **Financial Value:** It is typically the monetary value that is depicted in the company's financial statements. This value is particularly crucial for investors seeking a return on their investments. Companies create financial value by evaluating discount rates, return on equity, and costs of capital.

2. **Perceived Value:** It is a subjective value that is depicted in employee satisfaction, customer loyalty, brand trust, etc. Companies drive perceived value creation by implementing sustainable business practices, ensuring effective branding, offering top-notch customer support, etc.

Business leaders who wish to boost their company's profits and achieve long-term success must understand how to create both financial and perceived value for their stakeholders.

## DEFINING VALUE CREATION IN BUSINESS

Value creation is fundamental for every successful business, especially the MNC mindset backing them with the increased trust of customers, employees, and investors and the business's increased bottom line or profitability. Let's understand the value consideration for customers, employees, and investors!.

**Value Creation for Customers**

In the form of innovating the process, and understanding what they actually want.

**Value Creation for Employees**

By appreciating their work providing meaningful work, and good compensation plans, medical compensation plans, medical facilities, salaries, and perks.

**Value Creation for Investors**

In the form of increased profit margins, and increased business revenue and growth.

Every business cultivating an MNC mindset should consider value creation to enhance their business performance and transition into an MNC. MSMEs can revive their business or reach heights to become MNCs with the importance of value creation. Here, understanding the importance of value creation is essential!

## Start With the Mindset of Creating Value for Others

If you wish to become a multinational corporation (MNC), you cannot afford to be just another commodity in the market. You must go above and beyond the requirements of everyone in your chain of operations, Be it your customers, your employees, your vendors, or your collaborators. All your stakeholders must receive beyond expectations. Successful businesses create value with each transaction.

## Why is value creation important?

Value creation is one of the core mantras of success. It is the foundational bedrock of business. It's what sets you apart from your competition, fosters customer loyalty, and gives your Enterprise a distinct identity and branding. It is the starting point of any and every business transformation.

Every MSME looking to transition into an MNC dreams big to attain their goals, which can be done through value creation. The primary reason for MNCs' success throughout their journey and increased profitability stays within the value creation as it is crucial. Value creation is vital because it helps to stay in the long run and keep sustainability. Now you may be thinking about how companies perform value creation.

## How do MNCs Create Value?

MNCs create value to stay ahead in the following ways:

➢ Innovation and product development:

➢ Enhanced operations

➢ Customer-centric approach

➢ Expanding market globally

➢ Talent Management

➢ Collaborations

➢ Corporate social responsibility

## Benefits of Value Creation in Business

Value creation allows businesses to:

➢ Optimize activities to maximize output

➢ Create cost advantages over competitors

- ➢ Minimize organizational expenses
- ➢ Identify inefficiencies and take corrective actions
- ➢ Create a culture of high-performance
- ➢ Motivate employees to perform better
- ➢ Increase employee retention
- ➢ Improve product development
- ➢ Drive increased return on investment
- ➢ Enable optimum utilisation of resources
- ➢ Establish enhanced cooperation and coordination among teams
- ➢ Increase productivity and efficiency

Value creation enables you to position your organisation strategically in the market, ensuring long-term success and relevance. It is what sets you apart from your competition and brings distinct meaning to your brand and your products and services.

If you shift your focus from **'creating profit'** to **'creating value'**, chances are you will earn more profit than you are making now. So, focus on creating value and everything else will follow.

# CHAPTER - 6

# Navigating Success
## The Crucial Role of Knowledge Management in Transitioning from MSME to MNC

### KNOWLEDGE MANAGEMENT

Effective knowledge management plays a crucial role as you navigate the path of transitioning from an MSME to an MNC. Knowledge management involves systematically managing your knowledge assets to improve organisational performance and productivity. In this article, I will discuss the key strategies, challenges, and benefits of knowledge management in the context of this transition.

## Why is Knowledge Management Important for Business Growth?

Knowledge management creates a system to capture, organise, and utilise knowledge, enabling you to adapt, innovate, and thrive. As an MSME expands, managing and leveraging knowledge assets becomes even more critical.

## Leveraging Knowledge for Successful Transitioning

Knowledge encompasses expertise, experiences, best practices, and lessons learned from stakeholders and employees. By capturing and sharing this knowledge, you can develop a learning culture, encourage innovation, and adapt to new market demands.

## Conducting a Knowledge Audit

A knowledge audit helps identify existing knowledge assets and assesses their management practices, strengths, and weaknesses. Insights from stakeholders, employees, and subject matter experts are valuable in conducting this audit. Once completed, determine the most effective ways to capture and utilise these valuable assets.

## Mapping Knowledge Sources and Flows

Mapping knowledge sources and flows ensures seamless knowledge transfer and sharing across departments and individuals. This process helps identify bottlenecks, streamline knowledge-sharing processes, improve collaboration, and reduce redundancy.

## Capturing Tacit Knowledge

While explicit knowledge is easily documented, capturing tacit knowledge, which resides in people's experiences and minds, is highly valuable. Encouraging open communication and knowledge-sharing initiatives, such as mentorship programs and cross-functional collaborations, can effectively capture tacit knowledge.

# Knowledge Management Strategies for Successful Transition

➢ **Building a Knowledge-Sharing Culture:** Promote a knowledge-sharing culture by creating platforms for idea-sharing, collaboration, and open communication. Encourage teamwork and collaboration across the organisation.

➢ **Implementing Knowledge Capture and Documentation Methods:** US companies are very strong at this; this eliminates any personal biases and fluctuations. Establish a system for documenting best practices, standard operating procedures, and lessons learned—leverage technology tools to facilitate knowledge capture and retrieval and develop protocols for updating knowledge assets.

➢ **Cultivating a Learning Culture:** Nurture a learning culture through training programs, professional development opportunities, and recognition of knowledge-sharing efforts. Embrace a continuous learning mindset to adapt to new challenges and stay ahead.

➢ **Knowledge Localization:** Adapt to local knowledge and practices as you expand into different regions or countries. Incorporate local knowledge into your overall knowledge management strategy to operate effectively in diverse markets.

➢ **Facilitating Knowledge Sharing and Dissemination:** Establish communities of practice and cross-functional teams to promote knowledge sharing and dissemination. Create spaces for employees to connect, collaborate, and learn from each other.

> ➢ **Integrating Technology for Knowledge Management:** Implement knowledge management systems (KMS) to centralise knowledge repositories, making information easily accessible to employees. Integrate the KMS with systems like customer relationship management (CRM) and enterprise resource planning (ERP) for enhanced knowledge accessibility and utilisation.

## In Conclusion

Effective knowledge management is key to successfully transitioning from an MSME to an MNC. You can achieve adaptability, innovation, and growth by strategically assessing, capturing, and leveraging organisational knowledge. Develop a knowledge-sharing culture, leverage technology, and continuously evaluate the impact of knowledge management initiatives. Leverage the power of knowledge management to navigate your journey to becoming a thriving MNC.

# CHAPTER - 7

# Building Trust-Based Relationships Globally
# A Cornerstone of Growing from MSME to MNC

## TRUST: THE SPRINGBOARD TO YOUR MNC LEAP

Transitioning from an MSME to an MNC is about expansion, growth, and global reach. Among the most critical factors for growing into an MNC from an MSME is the ability to build trust-based relationships with global stakeholders.

Imagine your small business expanding beyond borders, transforming into a multinational company. This exciting journey isn't just about numbers; it's about trust. As you become a global player, building trust-based relationships becomes essential. In this article, I will discuss why trust matters, share easy strategies using real-life examples, and highlight how trust benefits your growth from MSME to MNC.

## Understanding the Concept

When we talk about building trust-based relationships globally, we mean establishing a bond of confidence with partners, clients, and stakeholders from different parts of the world. It's like a local shopkeeper who knows his regular customers' preferences transitioning to an online store and trying to understand the likes and dislikes of a global clientele.

## Why is Global Trust Crucial for MSMEs?

Trust is the foundation upon which successful international business relationships are built. When you are dealing with different languages, cultures, and rules, trust helps everyone work together smoothly. In a global context, trust becomes the glue that binds organizations, partners, and customers together. As an MSME grows into an MNC, the ability to bring trust becomes crucial, as it directly impacts reputation, collaboration, and sustainable growth.

➢ **Expanding Client Base:** Just as our local shopkeeper needs to gain the trust of global customers, MSMEs need to ensure potential international clients can rely on them.

➢ **Attracting Global Partnerships:** Trust facilitates collaborations and partnerships. A small tech firm in India might collaborate with a firm in the U.S. if they trust each other's capabilities.

➢ **Navigating Cultural Differences:** Trust helps in understanding and respecting the varied cultural nuances, ensuring smoother business operations.

## The Value of Trust in the MSME to MNC Journey

➢ **Brand Reputation:** Trust enhances brand reputation. A small toy manufacturer from Spain can become a favourite among Japanese customers if they trust the product's safety and quality.

➢ **Competitive Edge:** In a global market, businesses with a trustworthy reputation often have an edge over competitors.

➢ **Sustainable Growth:** Trust ensures long-term relationships, leading to sustainable growth. A software company from Brazil with a trustworthy reputation might retain a client from Germany for years.

## Easy Strategies for Building Trust-Based Relationships Globally

➢ **Cultural Respect and Learning:** As you expand globally, understanding and respecting the cultural nuances of each region is essential. By being culturally sensitive, you not only avoid potential missteps but also demonstrate a genuine interest in forming meaningful, trust-based relationships with local stakeholders.

Imagine you're starting to sell your products in a new country. To build trust, take time to learn about their culture. Understand how they do business and how they communicate. For example, when McDonald's entered India, they respected local customs by introducing a menu with no beef, respecting Indian values.

➢ **Honest and Clear Communication:** Open and clear communication is the backbone of trust. By establishing robust communication channels, you allow for feedback, address concerns promptly, and show that you value the opinions of your global partners and consumers.

Clarity and integrity are the two virtues that are of utmost importance when you want to build trust. Always share information openly, even if it's not good news. For instance, when Apple faced battery problems in some iPhones, they admitted the issue and offered solutions. This honesty helped build trust with their customers.

➢ **Keeping Promises: Consistent Quality and Service:** Consistent efforts to deliver the promised quality of products and services lead to creating trust among stakeholders, investors, buyers, clients, and all those related to your business.

To develop your strong reputation and trustworthy brand, you have to make sure that you maintain global standards for your products and services every time.

Imagine if you promised to meet someone for lunch but didn't show up. The trust would be broken. In business, it's similar. Keep your promises, whether it's delivering products on time or providing quality services. Amazon, known for its fast delivery, keeps its promise to customers, building trust every day.

➢ **Transparency in Operations:** Being transparent in your dealings, operations, and processes, you strive to create an environment of trust. Transparency is expected at any level of business; it is crucial when you foray into the global stage for better collaborations and partnerships.

➢ **Long-Term Perspective: Long-term Vision:** Building trust is not a task that you can add to your To-Do list. It is a journey that involves your values and vision. Have a long-term perspective when dealing with partners and stakeholders globally.

Do not run behind short-term gains; work towards nurturing relationships over time with strong dedication and commitment. Try to become reliable not just with words but with your actions. Building trust is like planting a tree. It takes time to grow strong. When you're working with partners from different countries, think long-term. Don't rush for quick gains.

> **Solving Problems Together: Collaborative Growth Mindset:** Growing globally is not just about expanding your brand but also about helping your partners grow. Adopting a collaborative mindset ensures that you're building relationships that are mutually beneficial. Imagine you're building a puzzle with a friend. If you both work together, it's easier, right? In business, facing challenges together creates trust.

> **Ethical Business Practices: Doing the Right Thing:** In the journey from MSME to MNC, ethics should never be compromised. Ethical business practices not only protect you from potential legal issues but also position your brand as one that values integrity over profits. Follow the rules, respect patents, and treat everyone fairly.

## In Conclusion

For MSMEs dreaming of becoming MNCs, building trust-based relationships globally is not just a strategy; it's a necessity. It's the bridge that connects local expertise to global success. MSMEs can ensure a smoother, more successful transition into the global market as respected MNCs.

# CHAPTER - 8

# MSME to MNC:
## Leverage Strategic Technology Integration

MSMEs are the backbone of the Indian economy. But, for the country to scale growth on a global level, it is crucial that these MSMEs mature into MNCs.

## INTEGRATING TECHNOLOGY

One sure-shot thing that can help MSMEs in this growth transition is the "adoption of technology". As technology continues to evolve at a rising pace, MSMEs will have to adapt to them to compete with large corporations and global players.

*Dr. Abdul Kalam once stated, "Technology is the highest wealth generator in the shortest time possible if done in the right direction."*

This quote from the legend highlights the transformative potential of technology for MSMEs.

MSMEs need to adopt and integrate evolving technologies like Artificial Intelligence, Cloud Computing, the Internet of Things, and Data Analysis techniques in their day-to-day business operations to accelerate growth. Undoubtedly, harnessing the power of technology has become crucial for MSMEs to become the next big MNC.

## Aligning Technology with Business

In today's digital era, technology and business go hand in hand. MSMEs that do not embrace technology often fall behind their competitors. They also face challenges in terms of scalability, operational efficiency and market reach. To survive and vie with larger global players and overcome these growth hurdles, MSMEs need to implement innovative and creative technological strategies in their operations whether it is product development, business processes, or marketing strategies. MSMEs can achieve their full potential only by adopting the latest technology.

## How Technology is Transforming Businesses

Technology today is the most effective driver of success and is evolving & transforming on a daily basis.

Enabling technologies like AI, Block Chain and IoT are redefining the business landscape, especially for MSMEs.

➢ **Scaling Opportunities:** Technology enables MSMEs to overcome traditional growth barriers and scale operations rapidly and efficiently. It empowers them to expand their reach, eliminating geographical limitations and providing access to a global customer base.

➢ **Access New Markets:** By embracing evolving technologies, MSMEs can tap into newer markets and target specific customer segments, thus competing on a level playing field with larger enterprises and MNCs. This will help them drive growth and diversification.

➢ **Data-Backed Decision Making:** Technology plays a crucial role in enabling MSMEs to collect, analyze, and interpret valuable data. The concrete data insights gathered drive data-driven decision-making. Instead of relying on opinions and biased data, technology facilitates improved and informed decision-making. For instance, Customer Relationship Management (CRM) solutions enable MSMEs to store and manage customer data efficiently and deliver actionable insights to forecast future sales, support sales management, automate marketing and sales processes, etc.

➤ **Brings Automation and Reduces Errors:** Technology helps MSMEs to alleviate the need for human labour in many mundane tasks. It enables the automation of repetitive and time-consuming tasks and augments human intelligence. By reducing human involvement in processes, MSMEs also eliminate the chances of human errors.

➤ **Streamline Distribution Channels:** With the help of robust technology, MSMEs can optimise their distribution channels and make their distribution processes more cost-effective and efficient. For instance, Enterprise Resource Planning (ERP) systems simplify inventory management, and logistics management, and streamline supply chain operations for MSMEs. This improves their operational efficiency and puts them ahead of their competitors.

## Key Takeaway

In today's dynamic business environment, we cannot ignore the potential of technology to propel the growth of MSMEs and transition them into MNCs.

Technology empowers MSMEs to navigate challenges and achieve long-term success. It increases their market penetration, enhances productivity and increases competitiveness. By leveraging enabling technologies, MSMEs can divert their focus on delivering innovative solutions and value creation.

Remember the success of your business relies on its adaptability and agility to embrace new technology.

# CHAPTER - 9

# Innovation:
# The Key to Growing from MSME To MNC

## INTEGRATING INNOVATION

With everything changing in today's dynamic environment, the business world is also always rapidly evolving.

And one aspect that is inevitable is the continuous innovation. Innovation is the way that provides new solutions to emerging problems as older solutions are no longer applicable.

*In the business world, innovation is not just a catchword but a necessity,* especially for MSMEs aspiring to become MNCs. In this article, we will talk about a few basic aspects of innovation in business, how it is important, and how to integrate it into your business growth strategy.

## What is Innovation in Business?

Innovation in business refers to a unique solution to a particular problem. To understand it better, let's talk about creativity and innovation; both are required to find a solution. It is obvious that not all creative ideas are useful. While creativity is more about finding unique ideas, innovation is about finding useful ideas. At the same time, novelty is always required in innovation.

Innovation can be a strategy, product, service, or business model that is both useful and unique. Moreover, innovation does not need to be a great technological breakthrough; it can be a simple improvement in your existing services or products to align with new emerging customer needs.

## What are the Types of Innovation?

There are two types of innovation that can be categorized for all kinds of businesses.

➢ **Disruptive and Sustaining**

➢ **Sustaining Innovation**

This type of innovation paves the way for the improvement of a company's existing services or products. Also, there can be innovation in the current product line to justify the emerging needs of the existing customer base. It helps a business to get an edge in the competition.

➢ **Disruptive Innovation:** Disruptive innovation is of great value for a particular industry overall. It happens when a newer player comes into the market, challenging the existing companies by establishing some differentiating factor. It can be low-end disruption and new market disruption. Low-end disruption leads to companies targeting the bottom end of the customer base. New market disruption means creating a new market segment for the untapped customer base.

# A Different Aspect of Innovation: Process Innovation

For MSMEs transitioning to MNCs, integrating both sustaining and disruptive innovation is essential for maintaining their market relevance and driving growth. **Apart from this, process innovation is another aspect where innovation is not just limited to improving or creating products or services. It also works around improving processes,** like streamlining processes, integrating new technologies, and finding better ways of working to boost productivity and reduce costs.

## The Importance of Innovation

As discussed above, the business world is dynamic, and unforeseen challenges will always exist. In this scenario, innovation keeps you afloat. Here are a few reasons why innovation is crucial for your business.

➢ **Promotes Adaptability:** Like during the COVID-19 pandemic, there was an immediate and imperative need for businesses to innovate in response to rapidly changing and unforeseen market needs. Those who embraced innovation thrived, while others struggled.

➢ **Leads to Growth:** It is detrimental to your business if you do not grow or stagnate at a particular point in today's market scenario. Innovative processes often lead to increased efficiency, reducing costs, and improving the bottom line. Innovation drives organizational and economic growth, keeping businesses afloat and thriving.

➢ **Gives an Edge in the Competitive Market:** In industries full of competition, innovation sets businesses apart, offering unique value propositions to customers. It develops a strong base for your business.

➢ **Improves Reputation:** Companies known for innovation are often seen as industry leaders. This reputation can attract customers, partners, and talent.

## Final Note

Innovation can be the driving tool for the growth of your business. However, there can be a few challenges on this path, such as resource allocation, associated risks, cultural shifts, and more. For businesses on the journey from MSMEs to MNCs, embracing innovation is not just a choice but a necessity for sustainable success and market leadership.y.

# CHAPTER - 10

# Differentiation: Standing Out in a Competitive World

> ## STANDING OUT FROM THE CROWD
>
> When you are treading on an ambitious journey to become an MNC from MSME, you need to stand out of the crowd to gain a strong position in today's highly dynamic business world.
>
> Here comes the role of differentiation, which is the strategic art of distinguishing your business from the competition. This article discusses different aspects of identifying and leveraging differentiators to scale your businesses globally.

What are the best aspects of your business? It may be the quality of your product, exceptional customer service, your innovative approach, or it may be your unique pricing plans. There definitely has to be something that sets you apart from your competitors.

## Identifying Key Differentiators for MSMEs

➢ **Know Your Target Market:** The first step for MSMEs is to get a thorough knowledge of their target market. What do your customers truly value? What are their specific needs and pain points? Conducting detailed market research and customer analysis is very important to get insights to help you shape your differentiators in a way that matches the needs and desires of your audience.

➢ **Competitor Analysis:** For global expansion, understanding the competition is crucial. To identify market gaps and opportunities, analyze both local and international competitors. You should gather information about what others are doing well or poorly. It will help you position your business strategically.

➢ **Unique Value Proposition (UVP):** Once research and analysis are complete, developing a unique value proposition is the most crucial step to position your business. It should clearly tell why your business is unique and how it solves customer pain points and addresses their needs better than others.

**Consider These Aspects When Crafting Your UVP:**

1. The specific problems your product or service solves.

2. How are your solutions superior to those of your competitors?

3. The unique features or benefits that your business offers.

➢ **Leverage Your Strengths:** Identify the most important offerings and achievements of your business. What are the best points of your business? It may be the quality of your product. If you offer exceptional customer service, you can take it as a differentiator. It can be your innovative approach, or it may be your unique pricing plans. It can be anything that makes your business stronger than the competition. These things can work as differentiators that will help your business to get an edge in the global market.

➢ **Craft Your Brand Story:** It is a fact that every business has a unique story, and yours does, too. Find your story and craft it in such a way that it connects with your audience at a personal, deeper level that it touches their emotions. Share your journey, mission, and values to build an emotional bond with your audience. This narrative will be your powerful tool in humanizing your brand and establishing trust. It will add to your unique positioning in the market, as each story is amazing.

➢ **Seek Continuous Customer Feedback:** Customer feedback is invaluable in understanding your business's positive or negative features. Gather customer feedback through surveys, interviews, and reviews. Customer insights can reveal what sets your business apart. Regularly collect and analyze feedback to identify what customers appreciate most about your business. This information helps strengthen your differentiators.

➢ **Stay Up to Date with Evolving Markets:** The business world is constantly changing. MSMEs must remain agile, continuously reviewing and adjusting their differentiators to stay relevant and appealing to their target audience.

## Align Your Differentiators According to the Target Segments

Here, it is essential to understand one more aspect: one differentiator may not appeal to different segments of your audience. Differentiators can be in different forms and can have varying impacts on different segments. Consider a few scenarios:

➢ **Technical Aspects:** For a technically inclined audience such as engineers, IT professionals, and others, highlight the advanced features of your product or service. Provide comprehensive information that underscores your offering's technical prowess.

➢ **Customer Support:** For audiences that value service, highlight your commitment to unparalleled customer support. Showcase your dedication to customer satisfaction and your responsive support system. Your audience should have enough confidence in your services that they can count on you in case any issues arise.

➢ **Financial Advantages:** For financial decision-makers such as CFOs, focus on the cost-effectiveness and economic benefits of your offerings. Be transparent by using clear data and demonstrate the financial advantages of choosing your product or service.

## Use Clear Communication

Craft your messaging in a way that resonates with diverse global audiences. Use language and terminology that they understand and appreciate. Highlight the benefits most relevant to them and simplify complex information to make it easier to understand.

## Use Pricing as a Differentiator

While pricing can be a differentiator, take up this approach with caution. Low pricing is not always a favourable approach as it can lead to a vulnerable position in the competition resulting in weak branding. So, in the case of Competitive pricing, consider value proposition, competition, and brand reputation, and all this without compromising the quality of your services/products.

## Final Note

For MSMEs on the path to becoming MNCs, differentiation is a strategic approach. It's about effectively communicating what makes your business unique and aligning these qualities with the needs of a global audience. Above all, differentiation is an evolving process that requires continuous adaptation and a deep understanding of diverse markets. By understanding the differentiation, MSMEs can position themselves for long-term success and stand out in the competition.

# CHAPTER - 11

# Research & Development:
## A Crucial Step to Go from MSME to MNC

In this chapter, we are discussing actionable steps for Small Businesses in India working towards Global Expansion.

## R & D YOUR CONSTANT COMPANION

Research and development are the most crucial aspects that you need to invest in even before you start with your idea of expansion.

It helps you understand customer needs and create or improve products and services to suit their needs.

**As I said earlier, you need to go to the basics for business transformation.**

For any business to transform, thrive, and sustain, you need to assess various aspects such as product/services, target audience, customers' requirements and aspirations, target markets, technology integration, risk management, cultural adaptability, cost reduction, revenue growth, and more.

If you do not put time and resources into research and development, your business will not achieve its goal and true potential. Businesses that keep exploring newer technologies and trends have better chances of growth and success than those that do not.

**So, what can you achieve through constant research and development efforts for your business?**

The benefits of R and D include important aspects such as product development, market strategy, operational efficiency, and competitive positioning, which are crucial for small businesses on the path to becoming multinational corporations.

Even small businesses understand the importance of research and development to grow and achieve their goals in this fast-growing business environment. This section will discuss practical and budget-friendly strategies for small businesses in India aspiring to become global.

## Starting Small with R and D

When we say R&D, we start thinking about labs, equipment, etc.

But R&D is not just about labs.

**It is about understanding people, products, needs, and aspirations.**

So, it may sound complicated, but starting it with small, manageable steps makes it result-oriented. You can begin by identifying areas where changes can be introduced in your current operations. This could be as simple as adopting new technologies to streamline services or improving a product based on customer feedback.

The objective here is to slowly introduce the R&D into daily operations so it does not strain your resources.

## Using Customer Insights for R&D

To gain Customer Insights, customer feedback is critical. Consumers these days are pretty active when it comes to sharing their feedback and their preferences. So, you can tap into this goldmine to understand your consumer. This approach is very practical in understanding the customer's mindset.

## R & D Does Not Mean A Huge Budget!

R&D is not always about big labs and huge investments. Yes, you can start it with a small allocation of your entire budget. You can start by taking simple steps, such as experimenting with new raw material suppliers to reduce costs or using more efficient manufacturing techniques. Make R&D a part of your regular business expenditure, not an occasional splurge.

## Take Help for Securing R&D Funding.

There are many funding options available for SMEs to carry on R&D. In fact, many government initiatives and schemes provide financial support for R&D activities. Also, you can explore crowdfunding and community funding as alternative financing methods.

## Protecting Your Innovations

R & D leads to innovation, and protecting your intellectual property is essential. You should understand the patent process. You can take the help of various consultancies and legal firms that can guide you through this process. By protecting your research, you can have a competitive edge.

## Use of Digital Tools for R&D

In this digital age, using various tools available to maintain pace in your R&D efforts is important. From online market research tools to social media platforms for gathering customer insights, you can get many insights. For instance, using data analytics tools to analyze consumer behavior patterns can provide valuable insights for product development.

## R&D for Global Market Fit

So, you are working to become an MNC.

Then, what is the most important information you need?

The basic thing you need to know is whether your product/ service fits global markets. To get this understanding, you need to research their culture, local markets, consumer behavior, and more so you can improve your offerings to match global standards and preferences.

## Tracking R&D Progress

Tracking your research progress is important. You can do it by setting up simple metrics such as tracking the impact of R&D on sales growth, cost savings, customer satisfaction, etc. Analyzing these metrics regularly helps you to take the right direction in your business growth.

## A Quick Reference Guide

**As a takeaway, here's a quick checklist for you to pursue the R&D journey:**

➤ Start small: Integrate R&D into daily operations.

➤ Utilize customer feedback for product/service innovation.

➢ Explore government grants and alternative funding options.

➢ Protect your innovations through patents.

➢ Leverage digital tools for market research and data analysis.

➢ Adapt your offerings for global market fit.

➢ Set up and track R&D metrics.

## In Conclusion

R&D is no longer a luxury reserved for big corporations. It has become a strategic tool for any business looking for expansion and carving out a niche in the global market.

The journey of R&D is continuous and evolving. Take small yet practical steps, and you can tread this path confidently and clearly..

# CHAPTER - 12

# Marketing Metrics:
# A Vital Navigator for MSMEs

## NAVIGATING SUCCESS WITH MARKETING METRICS

To run any business successfully, you must understand marketing metrics.

It becomes significantly more crucial for the sustained growth and success of the business while transitioning from an MSME to an MNC.

Marketing metrics help to monitor and assess the success of marketing efforts put in by a business.

Tracking marketing metrics helps in getting clarity about product reach, marketing penetration, and channel effectiveness. It helps in decision-making for the growth and sustainability of your business.

**Let us further discuss how you can understand and leverage marketing metrics.**

## Nurture a Marketing Mindset

Cultivating and nurturing a marketing mindset is about understanding the needs of your potential customers. The first step in this direction is to find your business's vision, mission, and values, where the primary goal is to satisfy your customers' needs and preferences.

At this point, focus on customer satisfaction scores, feedback, and reviews to understand the market pulse.

## Define Your Products and Services

Once the marketing mindset is cultivated, develop your products and services to cater to the market's demands and expectations. At this point, the metrics that help include sales performance, product performance, and customer usage metrics. These metrics help understand how your product or services are received in the market. It helps define areas of improvement.

## Find Delivery Channels

Delivery channels are the ways to deliver your products to your customers. It is very crucial to find out the best delivery channels. Channel performance metrics, delivery efficiency metrics, and customer reach metrics. These metrics help identify the most efficient channels to reach the customers and ensure a smooth delivery process.

## Understand the Market

When an MSME transitions into an MNC, it is essential to understand the market and the external environment where your business will operate, studying your competition. In addition, put effort into identifying the market trends and knowing customers' preferences.

You can get this kind of information through important marketing metrics, including market share, competitor analysis, and market growth rate. These metrics give complete insight into the market situation and help you identify opportunities and threats.

## Execute Marketing Strategies

Once all the important marketing metrics are gathered and analyzed, you can make decisions and develop marketing strategies to grow your MSME into an MNC. At this stage, the important marketing performance metrics include return on marketing investment (ROMI) and customer engagement metrics. With the help of these metrics, you can assess how impactful your marketing strategies are, and this helps make informed decisions for future marketing plans.

## The Bottom line

Marketing metrics act as a guiding force at every stage of your journey from MSME to MNC, from cultivating a marketing mindset to executing marketing strategies.

## Market metrics are more than just numbers.

They're the bridge between a marketing mindset and tangible business growth. By focusing on the right metrics, your business can grow on the path of success with confidence and clarity.

# CHAPTER - 13

# Unveiling the Power of Cost Intelligence

## A Deeper Look into Costs, Pricing, and Profitability

It is a real challenge for many organizations to figure out if their prices are trending in line with the market. And if they are not, what factors are leading to cost differences?

To get a deeper understanding of this, cost intelligence is the only solution.

## WHAT IS COST INTELLIGENCE?

Cost intelligence is a multi-dimensional cost and profitability modelling solution that conducts deep-dive analysis into costs, tracks market trends, forecasts recurring costs and maximizes alignment to the market.

It provides enhanced visibility into the costs, pricing and profitability of an organization.

It helps you delve into the past and gaze into the future by offering valuable analysis and insights into historical and forecasted cost trends.

> This cutting-edge model enables you to make more informed, confident and faster financial decisions.

If Indian MSMEs aim to venture into the global markets, they need to be cost-smart and beat the competition with cost intelligence.

## Cost Intelligence Caters to the Specific Needs of MSMEs

➢ It equips management with the tools to control costs effectively, optimize pricing efficiency, and enhance capacity.

➢ It helps navigate through economic uncertainty by gaining a comprehensive overview of avoidable costs, process inefficiencies, and the overall profitability of products, services, and customers.

➢ It helps anticipate future expenditure needs and pinpoint discrepancies between actual unit costs and desired targets or custom benchmarks.

## How Does Cost Intelligence Help MSMEs?

Cost Intelligence is the most powerful tool in the transformational journey of MSME into MNC. They offer data and insights to support cost reduction, performance improvement and risk management. It enables MSMEs to identify market-based risks and opportunities with the help of numerous effective cost models, qualitative market reports and cost trends. This empowers them to quickly understand and respond to market dynamics spanning regional, national, and international levels.

**Besides, cost intelligence brings forth a plethora of advantages for MSMEs, empowering them in multiple ways:**

➤ By harnessing data-driven insights, organizations can achieve significant savings through more transparent and informed negotiations with suppliers.

➤ Understanding the composition of costs related to purchased items and services becomes clearer and more accessible.

➤ With the ability to forecast and predict market-based cost risks, MSMEs can proactively navigate potential challenges.

➤ Unravelling cost trends over time is made possible by linking the underlying costs of items and services to relevant market indices.

➤ The identification of opportunities stemming from volatile market movements becomes more precise and targeted.

➤ Evaluating contract performance relative to market cost movements over time aids in making well-informed decisions.

➤ Leveraging relevant and granular indices assists in the formulation of pricing strategies with greater precision.

➤ Quick action is facilitated through access to numerous cost models, cost trends, and cost indices.

With numerous advantages, cost intelligence can help MSMEs establish their position in the global market and stay ahead of the competition.

## How Does It Work?

As businesses are advancing, the entire definition of Cost and Profit has changed.

> Today, Cost is not what we are incurring.
>
> Earlier, the sale/selling price was determined by the cost price and the profit desired, i.e.
>
> **Sale Price = Cost + Profit**
>
> However, today it is not that simple. Today you have to operate from a cost-based approach.
>
> Today you cannot randomly add any desired profit margin to your cost price and sell.
>
> Today your sale price is determined by what the customers are willing to pay, and what the competitors allow.
>
> **Cost-Based Approach, i.e. Cost = Market Determined Sale Price - Target Profit**

This means, if you have to increase your profit, you need to optimize cost.

## Cost Management and Profitability Solutions for MSMEs

Cost management and profitability solutions provide data-driven analysis to empower MSMEs to make strategic decisions around cost and profitability. It incorporates a scientific and data-backed cost and profitability analysis. It includes:

➢ **Cost Modelling:** Cost modelling is a powerful evaluation technique that helps businesses understand their cost structure and how money flows in and out. Through this lens, enterprises gain a comprehensive understanding of associated costs, benefits, and risks, thus providing insights necessary for making well-informed business decisions.

By delving into incurred costs, cost modelling reveals the true value derived from potential activities, acquisitions, or investments. It enables businesses to explore diverse scenarios, paving the way for the most cost-effective course of action.

Moreover, cost modelling acts as a vigilant detective, pinpointing cost inefficiencies that might otherwise go unnoticed. Armed with this intelligence, businesses can construct robust and practical cost models, ensuring optimal resource allocation and driving greater efficiency in their operations.

➢ **Cost Analytics:** Cost analytics is a well-established technique that empowers businesses to gauge the relationship between costs and associated revenue to estimate return on investment. By measuring the cost-output relationship, this approach provides valuable insights into the organization's cost incurred versus the benefits or improvements achieved in productivity.

Cost analytics identifies inefficiencies within the cost structures by conducting historical cost analysis. Based on the analysis, it helps organisations to rationalize and optimize costs. The cost-benefit evaluation aids in determining the most valuable alternatives in line with organizational priorities. It facilitates financial decision-making at top-level management.

In essence, cost analytics acts as a guiding light for businesses, enabling them to streamline costs and enhance overall efficiency.

➢ **Activity-Based Cost Management:** Activity-based cost management enables enterprises to analyze and evaluate their business activities using activity-based costing and value chain analysis. It is a proven technique to examine the cost of an activity viz a viz the value it adds to the overall operations.

This technique prioritizes value-generating activities thus resulting in improved customer experience and long-term profitability.

It is an effective tool for making pricing decisions. It drives enhancements in a company's strategic decision-making process by promoting economic efficiency in operations.

➢ **Continuous Cost Optimization:** Cost optimization is a business-driven approach that boosts performance, curtails expenditures, and achieves cost reduction, all while maximizing the overall value of the enterprise.

By embracing cost optimization, MSMEs can redirect saved resources to bolster their core competencies, facilitating substantial growth. Employing a structured cost optimization technique enables businesses to derive superior value from their investments, making them more appealing to potential investors for increased funding opportunities.

Cost optimization enables businesses to make informed decisions on where and how to cut costs and optimize their performance. This strategic technique empowers businesses to remain resilient during uncertainties, thrive in a dynamic marketplace and foster growth.

## In Conclusion

If you are seeking ways to identify cost savings, forecast cost risks or improve profitability, cost intelligence is your answer.

# CHAPTER - 14

# Mastering Cash Flow Dynamics for Business Growth

## THE IMPORTANCE OF CASH FLOW

Cash flow holds utmost importance for the success and sustainability of a company. It serves as the lifeblood of operations, representing the actual money coming in and going out of the business.

**Cash flow is more than just an accounting metric; it is a crucial indicator of a company's financial health.**

Understanding its significance allows businesses to make informed decisions, invest wisely, and navigate economic fluctuations with confidence.

By managing cash flow effectively, companies can ensure stability, growth, and adaptability, leading to triumph in the ever-changing landscape of opportunities and challenges.

**Therefore, ensuring a continuous flow of cash through your business is just as crucial for achieving success as generating strong profits.**

And you can only enjoy the rewards of success and profit if your business is capable of staying afloat through the rough times. Because it is ultimately the cash that keeps the business operations going, paying for supplies, labour and equipment. Besides, it is the cash that helps businesses expand and fulfil global ambitions.

Given the importance of cash flow in the business, it is essential to **Measure, Monitor and Manage cash flow.**

How do you do that?

## Keep your Cash Flow in Check

More than a third of small and medium-sized enterprises (SMEs) report cash flow issues as their growth barrier. Businesses must understand that cash flow is the pulse of their business and it is crucial for the health of their business.

Measuring, monitoring, and managing cash flow in a business are essential practices to maintain financial stability and propel growth.

➢ **Measuring Cash Flow:** Businesses must establish a robust system to measure cash flow by carefully tracking all incoming and outgoing funds. This involves analyzing cash inflows from sales, investments, loans, and other sources, while simultaneously monitoring cash outflows for expenses, overheads, and debt repayments. Regularly assessing the company's cash position helps identify potential cash shortages or surpluses, enabling proactive decision-making.

➢ **Monitoring Cash Flow:** Continuous monitoring of cash flow through financial statements and reports aids in understanding trends and patterns. It enables businesses to spot any deviations from projected budgets and take timely corrective actions.

➢ **Managing Cash Flow:** Effective cash flow management involves optimizing the timing of cash flows and employing prudent financial strategies, such as budgeting, expense control, and cash reserves, to ensure a healthy and sustainable financial position for the business.

## Consequences of Neglecting Cash Flow

Failing to measure, monitor and manage your cash flow poses significant risks to your business. It can leave your business with no liquidity to cater to unexpected expenses. It can result in insufficient inventory levels, which are vital for maintaining an uninterrupted supply chain. It can lead to financial troubles and hinder business growth. Therefore, maintaining a diligent approach to cash flow management is crucial to mitigating these risks and ensuring the sustained success of your business.

## How can SMEs Ensure Efficient Cash Flow in Business?

➢ **Work on Your Cash-to-Cash Cycle:** Cash-to-cash cycle, also known as the cash conversion cycle or order-to-pay cycle refers to the time it takes for a business to pay its suppliers for inventory and then receive cash from its customers. This metric basically indicates the time it takes for a company to convert its investments in inventory and other resources into cash flows from sales. Usually, the cash-to-cash cycle time benchmark is 30 to 45 days. The shorter the cycle, the better it is for business.

Cash-to-cash cycle analysis aids procurement and finance teams within organisations to identify issues in inventory, supply chain and collections processes and implement improvements to generate additional working capital.

Cash-to-cash cycle time reveals a lot about a company's operations and management efficiency. It also indicates the health of your supply chain. By monitoring cash-to-cash cycle time, you can enhance your cash flow management in the right areas to ensure less cash is tied up in operations.

As a business grows, customer demand increases. Selling more products means buying more inventory to meet demand, which ties up more cash in stock. Consequently, the amount of cash needed to bridge the time between spending on inventory and receiving sales revenue also rises. This can catch small businesses off guard and they can run out of cash. Therefore, maintaining a healthy cash-to-cash cycle time is especially important for small businesses to ensure they have sufficient money to pay operating expenses during the gap between purchase and payment.

To address cash-to-cash cycle issues, you can implement improvements in cash flow management, optimize inventory, negotiate better terms with customers and suppliers and streamline invoicing and payment processes.

## Work on Your Working Capital Cycle

Small businesses must also understand the working capital cycle, as it is an important financial concept. It helps you understand how long your money will be tied up in stock and inventory. In technical terms, it is the time taken by a business to convert net current assets and current liabilities (e.g. purchased stock) into cash. A long working capital cycle means the business has tied up capital for a longer time without earning a return.

The working capital cycle along with the cash flow statement can be anticipated to control the movement of funds into and out of your company, while also ensuring sufficient cash reserves to meet financial obligations.

It is crucial for MSMEs to understand their working capital cycle as it impacts the short-term financial health of the company and its capability to pay bills and fulfil financial obligations. A streamlined working capital cycle leads to improved cash flow management, enabling businesses to invest in growth opportunities, clear debts, and maintain positive supplier relationships. Understanding this cycle also empowers owners to make informed choices regarding inventory management and accounts receivable. This in turn reduces the financial strain and enhances overall financial stability.

Shortening the operating cycle of working capital is advantageous for your business. It allows you to use your cash to enhance the business instead of being stuck in the cycle. You can improve your working capital cycle by handling inventory smartly, collecting payments early, maintaining a shorter operating cycle and improving cash forecasting efficiency.

➢ **Evaluate Your CAPEX and OPEX:** You must perform a critical analysis of your CAPEX (capital expenditure, meaning major long-term expenses such as buildings, properties, machinery, vehicles, etc.) and OPEX (day-to-day expenses such as salaries, rent, utilities such as electricity, etc. and taxes) to determine where you can modify and optimize your cost and investment strategy and whether the returns are commensurate or not.

> **Conduct a Cash Flow Forecast:** A dynamic projected cash flow is an absolute must-have in today's fast-changing scenario. If the pandemic has taught us one thing, it is to be prepared for the worst-case scenario.

The capability of an organization to navigate through significant instability determines its long-term financial health. A cash flow forecast model serves as an early warning sign of a company's future business health by preparing for a variety of future circumstances.

Cash flow forecasting indicates whether a company has enough cash to run or expand its business. It helps businesses to anticipate cash flow bottlenecks and enables them to take proactive actions at an early stage to avoid cash flow gaps. Furthermore, it aids in better decision-making and setting measurable goals for business. Companies can do better cost control and receivable management with the help of efficient cash flow forecasting.

## In Conclusion

Effective cash flow management holds great significance for MSMEs, acting as the cornerstone of their financial success. By diligently monitoring and optimizing cash flow, these enterprises can ensure a stable and sustainable financial foundation, seize growth opportunities, and navigate challenges with confidence.

# CHAPTER - 15

# Benchmark with the Best: A Journey of Good to Great

In the quest to meet their ambitious targets, Micro Small and Medium Enterprises (MSMEs) often put on blinkers and focus on only reaching their predetermined goals. While this approach helps companies stay focused on their path, at the same time it restricts them from observing and learning from the ongoing developments in the business environment.

Instead of following this restrictive approach, MSMEs can adopt a more global approach which can help them stay in sync with the evolving market, competition and customer needs. But how?

Let us tell you!

## BENCHMARK WITH THE BEST

MSMEs can lead to the path of becoming Multinational Corporations (MNCs) by benchmarking with the best. It is a process of discovering the highest standard of performance within the same or different industry. It helps companies assess where they stand and how far they need to go to reach the top.

Benchmarking serves as a roadmap for MSMEs to help move forward and spread their wings. It involves comparing your company's business performance, processes, metrics and key performance indicators with the benchmarked company's business performance, processes, metrics and key performance indicators.

This comparison with industry bests helps understand the current best practices in your industry. More importantly, the learnings you gather can help implement improvements that can lead to better, faster, and cheaper outcomes.

## Benefits of Benchmarking

Benchmarking with the top companies at a global level can help MSMEs transform into MNCs and adopt best practices, ethical guidelines and working standards that provide the optimal course of action.

Benchmarking can help MSMEs navigate business challenges by identifying the problem areas or gaps and understanding the most effective resolution strategies based on the data collected from benchmarking and knowledge of best practices.

Furthermore, benchmarking helps organisations improve the quality of their products and services by observing current best standards and trying to match or even surpass them. It leads to better performance standards to remain competitive in the market.

Benchmarking provides organisations with insightful data that helps them implement the latest technology and efficient processes in their business which further leads to increased productivity and cost-efficiency.

## How Do You Benchmark?

The process of benchmarking involves five distinct steps:

> **Step 1 – Identify: Firstly,** you need to identify the areas that require improvement. It could be improving product quality, process improvement, reducing the cost of production, and boosting employee engagement, among others.

> **Step 2 – Plan:** Identify and shortlist the best benchmarking companies at a global scale and collect the data from these companies. Gather detailed information from several sources including primary and secondary sources.

> **Step 3 – Analyze:** Analyze the collected data to measure the performance. Identify the gaps between your performance and that of the benchmark.

> **Step 4 – Action:** Once you have identified the gaps, your next step is to devise improvements. Brainstorm ideas to effectively bridge the gaps. Create an action plan that clearly defines the goals and implement it.

> **Step 5 – Check:** Once the plan is implemented, closely monitor it to check if the changes are working as desired. If it is not working as expected, identify areas that need to be further improved.

## Benchmarking Doesn't End Here

While you can achieve improvements in your outcomes by benchmarking with the best, you need something else as well for successful benchmarking. You need:

> A continuous improvement mindset to foster innovation, efficiency, and adaptability.

➢ An active commitment to benchmarking from the management, employees and other stakeholders.

➢ A willingness to change and adapt in accordance with the benchmark findings.

➢ An openness to new ideas and innovation in existing processes.

## In Conclusion

By benchmarking with the best, you in turn can become the best benchmark for other companies who can look up to your organisation for best business standards and practices.

MSMEs that have successfully implemented benchmarking results have reported significant process improvements, productivity and cost savings.

Have you developed a comprehensive strategy for benchmarking yet to become a great company from a good company?

□ □ □ □

# CHAPTER - 16

# Simplifying Complexity:
## Harnessing the Effectiveness of Basic Solutions

> "The definition of genius is taking the complex and making it simple."
>
> ~ Albert Einstein

## BACK TO THE BASICS

Although we say 'keep it simple' on a daily basis, our minds are somehow conditioned into believing that, the harder we work to solve a problem or the more complex the approach we take to solve a problem, the more effective the solution will be.

## However, that is NOT ALWAYS TRUE!

Because of this belief that complexity is the answer to solving complex problems, we often completely disregard the simple solutions right in front of us and end up overcomplicating the situation.

> The same holds true for business scenarios too!
>
> You don't need comprehensive or complex solutions to solve complex problems. Instead, most complicated problems in business can be solved with very basic and simple solutions.
>
> All you need to do is go back to basics!

So if you are currently facing a problem in your business, this chapter is your cue to solve it by using simple ground rules that are very easy to understand instead of complex rules that can further complicate the situation.

## Applying Simple Solutions to Complex Problems

No matter how intricate or intertwined the problem might appear, simplifying it to its fundamental elements consistently reduces the intensity of the situation. This fundamental approach is another transformational mantra that all successful leaders and organizations use.

Let us understand this with a practical business example.

Let us say, your company shows a strong sales performance and impressive revenue figures. Despite boasting commendable profitability, your company is facing acute liquidity issues. You have insufficient funds to fulfill critical obligations. You are unable to promptly pay your vendors, compensate your employees, and manage existing liabilities. In a nutshell, you are facing a severe cash flow crunch which is significantly affecting your operational efficiency.

## Now what would you do to resolve your liquidity issues?

The fundamental rule says – to apply basic principles before anything else.

**In this situation, the basic solution could be:**

➢ Assess your working capital matrix.

➢ Thoroughly analyse your cash flow to understand where the money is going.

➢ Identify areas where you could cut back on costs like overhead expenses.

➢ Review your payment terms and negotiate with suppliers to get better terms.

➢ Monitor outstanding invoices closely and improve your accounts receivable management.

➢ Improve your inventory management to ensure your money is not stuck in inventory and to reduce storage costs.

➢ By applying the above-mentioned basic principles, you can overcome liquidity issues. As simple as that!

## Build a Transformative Transformation by Thinking Through the Fundamentals

Real transformation begins at the very foundation, where we address certain limiting beliefs that hinder our growth in relation to our true potential.

Once that is fixed, all you have to do is focus on fundamental transformations. These include deploying a customer-centric operating model, exploring growth verticals, exploring strategic tie-ups, driving innovation, using advanced analytics in day-to-day decision-making, embracing digital technologies and upskilling your workforce.

## Final Thoughts

Running a business is quite challenging as it is. Avoid adding unnecessary complexity by trying to solve problems in the most complex manner.

Effective problem-solving requires simple solutions. So, keep it simple!

# CHAPTER - 17

# Inspiring Success Stories of Indian MSMEs to MNCs

## 1. THE ADITYA BIRLA GROUP

### Building a Global Legacy from Humble Origins

The Aditya Birla Group is an Indian multinational conglomerate and a Fortune 500 company headquartered in Mumbai. In 1857, Shiv Narayan Birla laid the foundation of the Aditya Birla Group, which has since grown into a tremendous business empire.

The history of the Aditya Birla Group dates back to a cotton trading business established in the small village of Pilani in Rajasthan. With a fascinating journey spanning over 160 years, the group has grown into one of India's largest and most assorted conglomerates.

With its remarkable history and excellence, the group has not only left a mark on the Indian economy but has put India on the world map by focusing on globalization.

**With humble beginnings, the group today has a global presence and operations in 41 countries in Africa, Asia, and North and South America.**

**The Aditya Birla Group is a leading player in the market with a combined revenue of US$ 65 billion, of which over 50% of its revenue comes from its global operations.**

With thoughtful planning and a calculated move, the Aditya Birla Group gradually and successfully ventured into several business fields. Today, it is engaged in diverse sectors including metals, textiles and fibres, cement, fertilisers, chemical substances, financial services, agriculture, mining, telecommunications and more.

## Small Beginnings, Global Triumphs

Under the outstanding leadership of visionaries, the Aditya Birla Group achieved numerous accolades.

**The Group is among the first in India to establish a global footprint by setting up numerous manufacturing operations in Southeast Asia.**

Besides, it is a global leader in Aluminium Rolling, Viscose Staple Fibre and Carbon Black. In addition, it is the world's second-largest telecom company and India's largest telecom service provider. The group is also a leader in the Cement Industry in India.

## A Trustworthy Brand

Over the past 160 years, the Aditya Birla Group has solidified its reputation as a trustworthy and reliable entity. Keeping top-notch quality in its offerings, the Aditya Birla Group has won the hearts of people with its popular brands like Ultratech Cement, Grasim, Peter England, Pantaloons, Van Heusen, Idea Vodafone and Hindalco, to name a few.

The group has combined innovation with advanced techniques to create future-ready products and services to further enhance customer satisfaction and build a loyal customer base.

## Adaptability and Innovation

The Aditya Birla Group has been able to achieve significant milestones and attain global leadership in different business sectors owing to its ability to continually innovate to meet the varying needs of customers and the market at large. In order to stay relevant and competitive, the group emphasised adapting to changing times and market trends. By embracing innovation and adaptability, the group has successfully diversified and ventured into numerous sectors.

## Socially Responsible

The group strongly believes in giving back to society through various philanthropic initiatives and corporate social responsibility. The companies across the group have instilled a sense of mindfulness and a commitment to eco-friendly business practices that benefit the community and bring a sense of fulfilment and purpose. These initiatives in turn contribute to the growth and success of the group.

## 5 Growth-Driven Values

The Aditya Birla Group endorses its growth and success to its five growth-driven values that serve as a foundation of its actions. These values are:

- **Integrity:** The group defines integrity as honesty in every action and all dealing with customers, employees, suppliers, partners, shareholders and communities. The group is guided by fair and honest practices and the highest standards of professionalism.

- **Commitment:** The group defines commitment as doing whatever it takes to deliver as promised. It binds the group to provide value to consumers and stakeholders. Each employee as well as management takes complete ownership of their work and team as a whole. This value drives in creation of a results-oriented culture that is high on reliability and accountability.

- **Passion:** This value inspires and encourages the group to give its best. It facilitates building a culture of innovation and breakthrough thinking, resulting in increased customer satisfaction and value creation.

- **Seamlessness:** The group defines seamlessness as unity in thoughts and efforts. It involves thinking and working together in close coordination across hierarchy levels, functional silos, business lines and geographies. It illustrates teamwork, integration, empowerment, collaborative efforts and sharing across the group.

- **Speed:** The group defines speed as building an agile and proactive culture where the current and future needs of internal and external customers are responded to with a sense of urgency. It involves staying one step ahead always.

### The Bottom Line

The success story of the Aditya Birla Group serves as an inspiration for budding entrepreneurs and small medium enterprises that dream of becoming big multinational companies. With strategic planning and execution, the Aditya Birla Group has reached new heights of business, diversified its portfolio and expanded its worldwide footprint.

## 2. THE TATA GROUP: PIONEERING THE SME TO MNC TRANSFORMATION

### From a Small Enterprise to a Global Giant- The Inspiring Tata Group Success Story

The Tata Group is one of India's most successful and celebrated conglomerates, with over 150 years of remarkable history keeping the Tata flag flying high.

**Established in 1868 by Jamsetji Tata, the Tata Group built its story as a trading corporation with a mere capital of Rs. 21,000.**

**Today, the group has flourished from being a small trading company to a billion-dollar multinational corporation. In FY 2023, Tata Group reported a combined revenue of Rs. 12 lakh crore (US$ 150 billion).**

The group has made a mark in diverse industry sectors including steel, technology, telecommunications, auto, infrastructure, consumer and retail, financial services, hospitality, and more.

The group saw enormous growth and global expansion propelled through strategic acquisitions, partnerships, and investments. Currently, the Tata Group boasts a significant presence in more than 150 global markets across 6 continents, including Europe, Africa, North America, and Asia-Pacific. The renowned Tata Group owns a diverse portfolio of more than 100 companies across business sectors, including Tata Motors, Tata Steel, Tata Communications, Tata Consultancy Services (TCS), Indian Hotels Company, Titan, Voltas, Jaguar Land Rover, and many more notable names.

The Tata Group's success story goes beyond business.

## A Pioneering Brand

Tata brand boasts of excellent pioneering spirit. From establishing the first steel mill in India to providing the first branded salt in India, Tata established its strong base from the very beginning. Not just this, they also established the first power company in India and IT services company in India. They also pioneered establishing five-star hospitality in India, curating branded jewellery in India and having an international airline in India. They were the first to sell retail steel in India.

The Tata Group continues to diversify its interests and enter into various sectors by introducing new subsidiaries in the market.

## Innovation and Sustainability

Innovation and sustainability have been the driving force of the Tata Group since its inception. The group stays ahead of the curve by heavily investing in research and development, thereby encouraging creativity and new ideas across group companies.

**Furthermore, the group is crowned as a responsible corporate brand by contributing to sustainable practices and corporate social responsibility (CSR).**

The group's commitment to innovation, ethical business practices, and social responsibility has significantly contributed to attaining global recognition.

## International Approach to Business

Ever since its inception, the Tata Group has been global in its approach to business. They have always believed in implementing world-class technology and matching international standards in their product and service delivery. This approach has helped the Tata Group embark on an ambitious journey of global expansion in the last 20 years. It has transformed from an Indian brand to a successful global brand. In fact, a substantial portion of the group's total revenue is from overseas operations.

## The Tata Business Excellence Model

The Tata Business Excellence Model (TBEM) framework has been an integral part of organisational management practices in the Tata group. It is a robust framework that plays a pivotal role in fostering the growth of the Tata Group. It is based on the internationally renowned Malcolm Baldrige National Quality Award Model of the U.S. It provides a structured approach for assessing and improving various aspects of the business, including leadership, strategy, customer focus, and employee engagement.

By adhering to TBEM, the Tata Group companies can identify areas for enhancement, optimize processes, and enhance organizational efficiency. It helps the Tata Group companies to achieve excellence in their business performance and build globally competitive organisations.

This, in turn, results in improved customer satisfaction and increased competitiveness, driving overall growth. Through its systematic approach to excellence, TBEM continues to be a catalyst for the Tata Group's sustained expansion and success.

## Customer Centricity

Customer centricity has been the primary focus of the Tata Group. Where many companies today are grappling with growing customer expectations, pushing the boundaries to innovate and 'putting the customer first' has helped the Tata Group strengthen their brand, reinforce customer loyalty, achieve unprecedented growth and enhance performance.

## Strategic Planning

Effective strategic planning has allowed the Tata Group to adapt to changing market conditions and seize opportunities. The ability to not only develop comprehensive plans but also execute them has been a crucial factor in the group's growth. This approach has enabled the Tata Group to be agile and responsive to disruptions in a fast-paced market.

## Workforce Focus

The Tata Group truly understands the value of having a motivated workforce and therefore people focus has been their foundation pillar for success. The group demonstrates an unwavering commitment to creating and maintaining a top-notch workplace which is surrounded by talented and satisfied employees. Aligning efficient workforce practices with strategic goals has ensured that the right talent is in place to support the group's expansion.

## Process Management

Efficient process management has allowed the Tata Group to improve operations, reduce costs, and enhance the quality of their products and services. By embracing lean management techniques and agile strategies, they have responded effectively to market demands and changes, enabling growth through streamlined processes.

## Measurement, Analysis, and Knowledge Management

The Tata Group's emphasis on measurement and analysis has facilitated continuous improvement and innovation. By gathering and analyzing data, they have identified areas for enhancement, leading to better decision-making and ultimately contributing to organizational growth. Knowledge management has ensured that insights and best practices are shared and applied across the group companies, promoting efficiency.

### The Bottom Line

The Tata Group's success story is an inspiration to many small and medium enterprises that are aiming to become multinational companies.

# 3. THE GROWTH AND SUCCESS STORY OF THE MAHINDRA GROUP

The Mahindra Group is currently one of the largest industrial conglomerates in India with a presence across various sectors. However, its journey to becoming a multi-billion-dollar business empire started from very humble beginnings. Founded in 1945 in Ludhiana as Muhammad and Mahindra by three entrepreneurs - J.C Mahindra, K.C Mahindra and Malik Ghulam Muhammad, the group initially began operations in the steel manufacturing industry.

Over the past seven decades, through strategic decisions, innovative products and services as well as resilient leadership, the Mahindra Group has transformed and diversified into a global powerhouse.

**What started as a small steel trading firm is now a diversified group with over $19 billion in revenue and a presence in over 100 countries.**

This remarkable growth story is a testament to the vision and business acumen of the Mahindra family members who have led the group over the generations.

## Initial days

In the initial years after independence, the group focused on trading various types of steel under the name Mahindra & Muhammad. However, after the partition of India in 1947, Malik Ghulam Muhammad emigrated to Pakistan. The remaining promoters, J.C Mahindra and K.C Mahindra, changed the name to Mahindra and Mahindra in 1949. During this time, the group was primarily involved in manufacturing and supplying steel to the domestic market. A major turning point came in the late 1950s when the group decided to venture into automobile manufacturing by setting up an assembly unit for Willy's Jeep.

## Expanding Operations

A second-generation leader, Keshub Mahindra played a key role in transforming Mahindra & Mahindra into a full-fledged automobile manufacturer. In the 1970s, the company launched its first indigenously built passenger vehicle - the Mahindra & Mahindra 1500. This helped reduce dependence on Willys Overland and marked a turning point in the group's automobile business.

In the 1980s, under the stewardship of Keshub Mahindra as Chairman, the group underwent further diversification. New companies were formed in sectors like technology, infrastructure, finance etc. This helped the group spread its risk across industries. The tractor business also saw significant growth during this period with the launch of popular models like Mahindra 500 and Mahindra 60. By the 1990s, the group had established a strong presence across multiple sectors.

However, increased competition from global players posed new challenges. It was at this time that Anand Mahindra took over as Managing Director of the group's flagship, Mahindra & Mahindra.

The Mahindra Group further strengthened its position in India through organic growth as well as strategic acquisitions. Popular brands like Bolero, Xylo and Quanto further expanded their presence in the automobile market. The tractor business maintained its leadership position with new models tailored for domestic and international markets. Other group companies also grew from strength to strength in their respective domains.

## The Next Phase of Growth

By the 2000s, the group emerged as a leader in various sectors like tractors, utility vehicles, renewable energy, technology, hospitality and defence. Mahindra & Mahindra is the world's largest tractor manufacturer today. In 2018, Fortune India 500 placed it 17th on a list of the top Indian companies.

Under the leadership of Anand Mahindra as Executive Chairman, the Mahindra Group is now focused on the next phase of sustainable and profitable growth. New-age sectors like electric vehicles, clean energy and aerospace have been prioritized. The group also actively participates in corporate social responsibility initiatives.

The Mahindra Group's success story is a result of visionary leadership, business diversification, innovative products, strategic acquisitions and an ability to evolve with the changing market landscape over decades. As it embarks on its next phase of growth, the Mahindra Group is well poised to achieve greater heights and continue setting new benchmarks.

# 4. THE GROWTH STORY OF SUN PHARMA
## How it Transformed from an SME to an MNC

Sun Pharmaceutical Industries Ltd., which is currently one of the largest pharmaceutical companies worldwide, has enjoyed remarkable growth and transformation throughout its eventful journey of four decades.

**It has grown from a one-drug company to a pharma giant with revenues of over US$ 5 billion.**

Let us delve deeper into Sun Pharma's case of success and what made it possible for this SME to turn itself from a small Indian business struggling to catch up with its product market in the country, not even daring to export anywhere outside India to a big name in the industry today.

## The Early Days in Vapi

Mr. Shanghvi's father had a small medical representative firm in Kolkata that was involved with psychiatry drugs. This is how young Dilip had his first taste of the pharma business.

In 1983, supported only with Rs. 10,000 and a team of just five individuals to back him up, Sun Pharmaceuticals was established by Dilip Shanghvi in the industrial town of Vapi, Gujarat. Initially, they started by producing five psychotropic drugs and were more focused on creating niche brands developing targeted therapies that would appeal to doctors instead of chasing huge volumes. The company adopted a specialized approach to pharmaceuticals and it began paying off whereby in 1987, Sun Pharma already had a pan-India distribution network in place as annual revenues increased significantly.

## Rising the Ranks

In the 1990s, Sun Pharma increased its growth greatly through enhanced research and development, new product introductions as well as exporting to more countries. It invested significantly in state-of-the-art global GMP-compliant manufacturing facilities and many of its products were approved in regulated markets such as the US. It became one of the early Indian companies to export formulations to regulated markets.

**In 1994, the initial public offer of 1.5 million shares by Sun Pharma was oversubscribed by a whopping 16 times. The offering raised Rs. 28 crores.**

In 1996, two years later the company established an Overseas Subsidiary and expanded to cover 24 countries within Europe as well as the USA. In 1997, there was a major boom as the annual revenues rose to Rs. 180 crores.

## Landmark Acquisitions and Consolidation

The new millennium was a breakthrough stage when Sun Pharma launched its acquisitions business and determined inorganic growth as the best way forward.

**However, the boldest move was when it overtook Sun Pharmaceutical Industries to become the largest Indian drug maker, contributing to becoming even larger with its US$4 billion acquisition of Ranbaxy Laboratories in April 2014.**

It portrays strong visionary and strategic leadership skills in Dilip Shanghvi who bought a sick Ranbaxy at a good discount and brought it again on track. Later acquisitions were Taro Pharmaceutical and Icon Plc.

## Riding the Global Growth Wave

Innovation is also part of the company which explains why in the recent past it was consistently achieving strong financial performance based on inputs like niche therapies or entry into fast-growing pharmaceutical markets such as Brazil, China, Russia and Africa. This has facilitated a 20-fold growth of Sun Pharma's revenue from the year 2000 to over Rs. 30,000 crores currently.

## Leadership Through Tech and Sustainability

In the long run, Sun Pharma is looking at sustainability in terms of advanced technologies including Artificial Intelligence, Machine Learning and Process Automation as a way to sustain itself within leadership. One of their sustainability practices includes energy and water usage reduction, minimization of waste, etc. Even today, the diverse portfolio of their high-quality and affordable medicines touches millions of lives all over the world including in the Americas and Europe, apart from Asia and emerging markets where they gained leadership.

# 5. THE RISE OF AN INDIAN TECH GIANT
## The Infosys Growth Story

Infosys started small in 1981 but now leads technology worldwide. This was made possible because its founders, big ideas and strong leadership helped it grow fast. Infosys also planned well for the future while keeping up with challenges along the way. Infosys was started in Pune, India by seven smart business people - N.R Narayana Murthy, Nandan Nilekani and others who wanted to make India known as a place for worldwide technology skills. Below is its story of growth and resilience.

## The Beginning

**Beginning in a rented place in Pune with only Rs. 10,000 as starting money - borrowed from Narayana Murthy's wife - Infosys started as a small business ready to make its name known worldwide.**

In the first years of the 1980s, it was new and not completely tested to send technology work from India overseas. However, the visionaries who started it still strongly believed that India could become a reliable place for making computer programs around the world. Their vision helped people worldwide slowly see India's skills in IT.

## Narayana Murthy's Leadership

An important thing that helped Infosys grow fast was the new Global Delivery Model adopted by Murthy as a leader. This new idea used skilled people from affordable places in India to provide expensive computer services at a low cost. The people who started this knew that sharing resources around the world would greatly cut costs for customers while still keeping high-quality service. With multiple places of operation like Pune, Bangalore, etc. Infosys could grow fast to deal with more client demands.

## Focus on Quality

To ensure strict compliance with quality standards that global clients demanded, Infosys heavily invested in training programs and technical upgrades. These initiatives laid the foundation for Infosys to gain the trust of top corporations as a credible partner.

Some of Infosys' earliest clients in the 1980s-90s included big names like IBM, Arthur Andersen, Tata Motors and L'Oreal.

**As the 1990s progressed, Infosys became one of the first Indian companies to list on a US stock exchange through its IPO on NASDAQ in 1999,** attracting further international attention.

## Digital Transformation and Global Expansion

Over the decades, Infosys consolidated its leadership in technology services by expanding its service portfolio from just software development to new-age digital capabilities like Cloud Computing, Artificial Intelligence, Machine Learning and more. It also made strategic acquisitions to boost these focus areas. Under the visionary leadership of former CEOs like Murthy, Nilekani, Gopalakrishnan and Shibulal, Infosys grew to become a Fortune 500 Company with a global workforce exceeding 250,000 across 50 countries by the late 2010s. From serving just 6 clients at inception, Infosys' client portfolio expanded to over 1000 global corporations by the present day.

## Infosys Today

While steadfast commitment drove Infosys' rise, the journey was not without its share of challenges, the first of which came early on in 1989 with the failure of its joint venture in Saudi Arabia named KSA Infosys. The dot-com bust of 2001 posed another threat that Infosys overcame under Nilekani's leadership, emerging stronger through prudent operational strategies. Infosys also faced cultural adaptation challenges from expanding globally and acquiring new companies. Its commitment to quality, client relationships and employee welfare helped it successfully overcome such hurdles through the years.

**Today, Infosys has made its name as a top Indian IT brand worldwide with more than $100 billion in value.**

Its amazing journey is a shining example of endurance, new ideas and how planning smartly can help an Indian startup become successful around the globe.

# CONNECT, CONVERSE AND CO-CREATE WITH THE UNIVERSE

'In the pages above, I have shared with you the gateway to the portal of progress and transformation. Following and implementing these super tips and life-altering practices will set you firmly on the path to manifesting your dream of turning your MSME into an MNC.

Before we move on to the next section of the book dedicated to "Testimonies of Truth" from people who have already experienced this magic and fulfilled their dreams under my mentorship, I have one more gem of wisdom to share with you.

Remember that all worldly, material and financial transformation is possible only when you are spiritually anchored; when you know that you are here for a purpose, then all universal energy supports you unconditionally in fulfilling that purpose.

And believe me; this is no new-age mambo jumbo- science has proven what spirituality has always proclaimed; that everything is energy and the universe functions through the language of vibration.

Therefore spend some time in meditation and introspection every day to sit and **connect with the universe.**

In this deep state of connection, the intuitive guidance and advice you receive as thoughts are invaluable; This is how **the universe converses with you.**

Ensure that you act on this intuitive guidance you receive because when you take guided action, you attract what you desire. The universe then sends you abundant support in the form of opportunities, people and resources etc. **This is how you co-create success and abundance with the universe.**

So take a few deep breaths to centre yourself and begin practising and implementing all that I have shared in this book so that your success story can be a part of the next edition of this book in the *"Inspiring Success Stories"* section...

# TESTIMONIES OF TRUTH– YOU COULD BE NEXT!

n this section, I am sharing with you a few of the innumerable real-life transformational experiences that my clients & I have created as a team.

These are shared with the sincere intention of inspiring you to take action toward your dream/goal of journeying from an MSME to an MNC.

## Unparalleled Expertise- Invaluable Guidance

"I cannot say enough good things about the Global MSME & Realty Strategist and his mentorship services.

His guidance has been invaluable in helping me understand the financial aspects of running a business and creating a Purpose Driven Enterprise.

He has a unique ability to break down complex financial concepts into understandable and actionable steps, which has helped me make better decisions for my business.

The coach's commitment to helping his clients succeed is truly remarkable, and his expertise in financial management and strategy is unparalleled. If you're looking to grow your business and create a lasting impact.

I highly recommend working with this coach."

~Arvind Singh, Managing Director,
Krasa International Pvt. Ltd

## Sky-High Commitment & Care For Clients

"I had the pleasure of working with the Global MSME & Realty Strategist for over a year, and I can confidently say that my business wouldn't be where it is today without his guidance.

His focus on creating a Purpose Driven Enterprise has not only helped us increase our profits but has also given our company a deeper sense of meaning and impact.

He truly cares about his clients and their success, and I would highly recommend his mentorship services to anyone looking to take their business to the next level."

**~Ashish Kaushik**

**Entrepreneur**

## Increased Income & Impact Exponentially!

"I highly recommend the mentorship services of this Global MSME & Realty Strategist for any business owner looking to not only increase profits but also create a purpose-driven enterprise.

With his expert guidance and support, I was able to develop a financial strategy that aligned with my business goals and values.

He provided me with invaluable insights into financial planning, budgeting, and forecasting and helped me identify areas for improvement in my business operations.

His approach is highly personalized and tailored to my specific needs, and he is always available to answer any questions and provide ongoing support.

Thanks to his mentorship, my business is not only more profitable, but it is also making a positive impact on the world. I cannot recommend their services enough!"

~Rajesh Jain

**Director Arihant Infrra Realtors Pvt. Ltd.**

**Using the strategies shared in this book, your testimony could be a part of this section in the next edition of this book.**

The time to take action toward your dream of building a purpose-driven global enterprise is NOW! ***Let's Start Your Journey To Build MNC***

**Reach out for a free one-to-one discovery session at:**

M: 9312213765

E: pjainonline@gmail.com

W: CmaPankajJain.in

9 789363 380110